Competitive Advantage: Linked Management Systems

Gail and Neil

You've been great friends over the years. We know we can always count on you.

If you have trouble sleeping take this book to bed.

Sandy

Competitive Advantage: Linked Management Systems

Sandford Liebesman, Ph.D.

PROFESSIONAL

Chico, California

Most Paton Professional books are available at quantity discounts when purchased in bulk. For more information, contact:

Paton Professional
A division of Paton Press LLC
P.O. Box 44
Chico, CA 95927-0044
Telephone: (530) 342-5480
Fax: (530) 342-5471
E-mail: *books@patonprofessional.com*
Web: *www.patonprofessional.com*

ISBN: 978-1-932828-35-1

Library of Congress Cataloging-in-Publication Data
Liebesman, Sandford, 1935-
Competitive advantage : linked management systems : financial, quality, environmental, and IT management working together to improve the bottom line / Sandford Liebesman.
    p. cm.
 Includes bibliographical references and index.
 ISBN 978-1-932828-35-1
1. Management information systems. 2. Corporations--Finance. 3. Total quality management. 4. Environmental management. 5. Industrial management--Philosophy.
I. Title.
 HD30.213.L54 2011
 658.4'038011--dc22
                    2011007633

Notice of Rights

Notice of Liability

Staff
Publisher: Scott M. Paton
Editor: Laura Smith
Book design: Scott Sleeper
Cover: Scott Sleeper

DEDICATION

I want to dedicate this book to my wife, Elinor. She exhibited a great deal of patience with me during those many late hours at the computer and acted as the first line editor of my publications.

Contents

Preface

This book illustrates how organizations can link their quality, environmental, financial, and information technology management systems and describes the benefits of these systems working together. Unfortunately, modern business management systems don't usually communicate well. They behave like independent silos,[1] which results in less-than-optimal operations, excessive costs, and unhappy customers and investors.

Why do I use the term "linking" in this book in stead of "integrating"? Integrating usually means that one management system dominates while the others lose their identity.

Quality and environmental managers need to understand the language of finance and the effect of operations on the bottom line, and financial managers need to know how quality and environmental managers can help improve results. The message is that each of these managers needs to understand what the other brings to the table. The long-term advantages of this cooperation will be cost savings, continual improvement of processes and products, and a greater understanding of each other's work and responsibilities.

The book is based on work I did linking ISO 9001 and ISO 14001 to compliance to the Sarbanes-Oxley Act (SOX).[2] This included publishing articles in *Quality Progress* and other publications; leading two American Society for Quality conferences on SOX; presenting eight SOX workshops; and interacting with financial professional societies such as the American Institute of Certified Public Accountants, the Institute of Internal Auditors, the Sarbanes-Oxley Institute, and the Institute of Management Accountants. It became evident during my efforts that the topic was much broader than compliance to a law, so I expanded my outlook to the larger issue of effective overall management of an entire organization. Linking management systems will improve effectiveness of the organization and customer satisfaction and will have a positive effect on the bottom line.

The book is divided into two parts. The first part, chapters 1 through 5, provides the background needed to understand the linking philosophy. The second part provides information on implementing linked management systems.

---

1. Sandford Liebesman. "Down with Silos," *Quality Progress*, September 2008, 64–67.
2. The Sarbanes-Oxley Act of 2002, The U.S. House of Representatives, HR 3763, July 24, 2002.

Chapter 1, "Linking Management Systems," introduces quality and environmental managers to the language of finance and describes the effect of operations on the bottom line. I also indicate how quality and environmental managers can work with financial managers to improve the organization's results. In this chapter I introduce the roles of ISO 9001 and ISO 14001, Lean Six Sigma, and information technology in a linked management environment.

Chapter 2, "QMS/EMS Support of the Sarbanes-Oxley Act," introduces SOX. I show how specific clauses of ISO 9001 and ISO 14001 support SOX section 404 compliance through the use of the Committee of Sponsoring Organizations of the Treadway Commission (COSO) guidance. I also introduce the idea that the six required documented procedures of ISO 9001 can be used by the other management systems.

Chapter 3, "Risk Management's Importance in Today's Economy," describes a common risk management methodology. This includes the organization's objectives, definition of risk categories, identification of risks to meeting the objectives, and methods for managing the risks. I introduce key functions of a risk management program: risk appetite, risk tolerance, the use of controls, and risk management tools.

Chapter 4, "The Importance of Information Technology in Effective Business Operations," discusses the role of information technology in an organization. I describe IT's support of SOX, management of controls, and information security. ISO 27001 and CobIT are two tools used to assure effective information security.

Chapter 5, "Linking Lean Six Sigma to Management Systems and Information Technology," describes the use of a Lean Six Sigma program to reduce the cost of finance, quality and environmental management, and information technology. I discuss some of the Lean Six Sigma tools and give examples of their use in management systems.

After finishing Chapter 5, the reader should have a good understanding of the individual management systems, supporting tools, and the philosophical background of linked management systems.

Chapter 6, "Implementing Linked Management Systems," describes the structure of a linked management system, provides an implementation process, and indicates what management must do to assure the effectiveness of the new system. There are discussions of key controls and their importance in auditing of the system. I describe audits of the management systems separately and integrated audits of the three systems together. I also discuss separate audits of information technology systems. Also in chapter 6, I describe a four-phase methodology for implementing a linked management system that consists of planning, development, internal assessment, and external auditing. The description includes deliverables for each phase.

Chapter 7, "Lessons Learned from Linked Management Systems," contains experiences of organizations that linked their management systems to comply with SOX section 404. Two sets of questionnaires were filled out by these organizations. The first describes how their quality organizations supported the financial auditors in their systems. The second provided more details on how the linked management systems were implemented. This chapter includes a linked management system story that illustrates how an organization can improve communication between quality and financial auditors and identified key results affecting the bottom line. Finally, there are examples of case studies from a new ISO book describing guidance on how to integrate requirements of multiple ISO and non-ISO management system standards.[3]

Chapter 8, "A Foundation for Linking Management Systems," defines a series of eight actions for linking management systems. The eight actions are: connect the management systems by using common processes; implement the ISO 9001 process approach in all management systems; where applicable, link operations to the SOX compliance process; implement continual improvement activities as defined in ISO 9001; ensure that the risk assessment process is complete and operating effectively; conduct linked audits; clarify the role of information technology; and improve corporate governance.

There are three appendices and a bibliography after chapter 8. The appendices are:
- Appendix A: Sarbanes-Oxley Act Index
- Appendix B: Case Studies
- Appendix C: Definitions and Acronyms

The bibliography contains lists of books, articles, and websites.

The intent of this book is to describe a methodology for breaking down the silos that exist in most organizations and linking management systems so they work effectively together. The benefits will accrue to the organization's bottom line and improve its overall operation.

---

3. *The Integrated Use of Management Systems*, International Organization for Standardization (ISO), Geneva, Switzerland, 2008.

Introduction and Acknowledgments

This book is the culmination of my work in new areas of quality management over the last eight years. I'm grateful to the many colleagues with whom I have worked.

My interest in linking management systems started in 2003, when Paul Palmes and I attended a presentation by Greg Hutchins in which he mentioned the then-new Sarbanes-Oxley Act (SOX) as a concern for supply management programs. Paul and I examined SOX and learned that its section 404 was the major issue. We then found the Committee of Sponsoring Organizations of the Treadway Commission (COSO) guidance and determined that ISO 9001:2000 could provide linkage from quality management to financial management in organizations' compliance efforts. Our colleagues John Walz and Donna Spencer joined us and we formed the American Society for Quality (ASQ) SOX team and the ASQ SOX community.

In November 2004, I attended an Institute of Internal Auditors course called "Sarbanes-Oxley Act: Implications and Impact for Internal Auditors," which was taught by Don Espersen. This was the start of my obtaining a more comprehensive view of financial management. I subsequently spent a great deal of time with Cecil Nazareth of the American Institute for Certified Public Accountants (AICPA). Cecil provided me with a valuable link between quality and financial management when I learned that the AICPA is ISO 9001 certified and that the standard is the basis of its overall management system

In 2004, we found that many organizations were linking their quality management systems to their SOX compliance efforts. Eight organizations agreed to complete a questionnaire we created describing the way they linked their management systems. The contacts who were highly supportive of the SOX team were Paul Palmes of Northern Pipe/OtterTail, Dirk Van Putten of Linear Technology, Donna Spencer of the Nordam Group, Dexter Hansen of NVE Corp., Jim McCormack of Communication Test Design Inc., Lindy Olson of Intrado Corp., Scott Bickley of International Gaming Technology, and Tom Carpenter of the StonCor Group Inc.

Dexter also introduced me to his website, which contains a great deal of supportive information.

A second questionnaire was completed by Dirk Van Putten, Donna Spencer, Dexter Hansen, Tom Carpenter, Tom Welsch of 3M Corp., and Jack A. Phillion of the Woodbridge Group. Andy Hofmann of Metrics Management Consulting Inc. worked with Jack on the questionnaire.

I want to thank several people who recently provided me with excellent case studies. Joe DeFeo and Linda Ellrodt of Juran Institute, who provided me with two case studies. One was on risk management at a teaching hospital and the second addressed design for Six Sigma (DFSS) and the define-measure-analyze-design-validate (DMADV) process for linking Six Sigma to financial management at a major U.S. cabinetmaker. Atul Dhanorker, quality management coordinator at the Mayo Clinic, provided a case study using define-measure-analyze-improve-control (DMAIC) to improve the operation of a warehouse in New Jersey as part of a class taught by Ed May. Dexter Hansen described the implementation of a linked management system at NVE Corp., and Tom Carpenter provided a similar case study on implementation at the StonCor Group Inc. Finally, Wes Rhea, professor at Kennesaw State University, provided a case study on information technology at a health management organization.

There were many other individuals who expanded my understanding of quality's linkages with financial management. Sanjay Anand, chairman of the SOX Institute, worked with me to develop a course on quality management and SOX. Jeff Thomson of the Institute of Management Accountants communicated with me during the review in 2006 and 2007 of the PCAOB auditing standard No. 5 and the new Securities and Exchange Commission (SEC) guidance. Others who provided valuable inputs were Shireesh Joshi of Crescent Consulting; Rochelle Goehring of Singer, Lewak, Greenbaum and Goldstein LLP; Jay Patel, chair of the Northeast Quality Council; and Will Wang of the British Standards Institute. Greg Hutchins of Quality Plus Engineering expanded my knowledge of business continuity and disaster recovery.

I also received support from Ed May of Maplewood Consulting, Mike Parillo of Loop Cable Works, and Carl Perini of ISP Corp., on the role of Lean Six Sigma in support of financial management, quality management, environmental management, and information technology.

I owe a great deal of thanks to Sue Daniels, my editor at *Quality Progress*. She suggested the title of my article in the September 2008 issue, "Down with Silos." Much of the material in the book was adapted from articles I published in *Quality Progress* and *Quality Digest*. Two other editors provided support and published my articles on SOX. They are Jim Mroz of *Informed Outlook*, and Paul Scicchitano of *Quality Systems Update*. I also want to thank my contact at Quality Press, Matt Meinholtz and my new editor Brett Krzykowski. Finally, I want to thank Laura Smith, my editor at Paton Professional, for an excellent job of helping me accomplish my goals for this book.

Chapter 1

Linking Management Systems

1.1 INTRODUCTION

There are many advantages of linking an organization's quality management system (QMS) and environmental management system (EMS) to its financial management system (FMS).

According to the internal control/integrated framework[1] developed by the Committee of Sponsoring Organizations of the Treadway Commission (COSO):[2]

> *The quest for quality is directly linked to how businesses are run, and how they are controlled. Quality initiatives become part of the operating fabric of an enterprise. These quality factors parallel those in effective internal control systems. In fact, internal control not only is integrated with quality programs, it usually is critical to their success.*

This book was written to illustrate how organizations can effectively link their quality, environmental, information technology (IT), and financial management systems and to describe the benefits of these systems working together. The linked system will be shown to support compliance to the requirements of the Sarbanes-Oxley (SOX) legislation.

This book will describe ways of improving the dialogue between financial, quality, IT, and EMS. Managers of these management systems need to understand what their peers in other departments do. Quality and environmental

---

1. *Internal Control—Integrated Framework,* Committee of Sponsoring Organizations of the Treadway Commission (COSO), published by COSO, 1992 and 1994.
2. Committee of Sponsoring Organizations of the Treadway Commission, Internal Control—Integrated Framework, September 1992 and May 1994. Committee of Sponsoring Organizations of the Treadway Commission, Internal Control—Integrated Framework Evaluation Tools, September 1992.

1

managers often don't understand the language of finance and the effect of operations on the bottom line, and financial managers need to know how quality and environmental managers can help improve bottom-line results. This understanding results in long-term cost savings, continual improvement of processes and products, and a greater understanding of each other's work and responsibilities.

1.2 OVERVIEW OF MANAGEMENT SYSTEMS

1.2.1 Quality management systems' strategic framework
An organization's QMS' strategic framework consists of:
- *A foundation.* The core purpose or reason for being is in the organization's mission statement, core values, and services.
- *Priority themes and guiding principles.* These are priorities for the future and provide strategic direction in advancing the organization toward its mission.
- *Mission statement.* The organization's mission statement should define its role in the industry. This should include a description of the products and services it intends to provide and how it will benefit its customers.
- *Core values.* The framework should include a definition of its core values, such as integrity and ethics, code of conduct, leadership, competence, customer responsiveness, sustainability, and quality principles.
- *Core services.* These should be defined for the organization in terms of the benefits to its stakeholders (i.e., customers, employees, investors, government, and society).
- *Strategic priority themes.* These should be developed to enhance the benefits to the organization's stakeholders.

The quality manual
An organization's quality manual should define its quality policies. The QMS defined in this book is based on ISO 9001:2008.[3] The implementation of a QMS enhances member and customer satisfaction and improves awareness of customer requirements.

ISO 9001:2008 promotes a process approach to develop, implement, and improve the effectiveness of an organization. This broadly consists of the application

---

3. *ISO 9001:2008 Quality management systems—Requirements*, International Organization for Standardization (ISO), Geneva, Switzerland, November 15, 2008.

of a system of processes, together with the identification and interaction of these processes and their management and improvement over time.

The quality manual should address the eight basic clauses of ISO 9001:2008. Clauses 1 through 3 describe the philosophy and application of quality management and include definitions and references. Clauses 4 through 8 outline the structure of a good management system:

- *Clause 4 (Quality management system).* Defines the process approach and documentation requirements, which include the quality manual and documented procedures for control of documents and records. The process approach requires identification of all processes and their application; determination of their sequence and interaction; definition of criteria and methods to ensure that processes are effective; provision of resources and information to support operation and monitoring of the processes; monitoring, measuring, and analyzing the processes; and implementing actions to achieve results and continual improvement and to ensure control over outsourced processes.

- *Clause 5 (Management responsibility).* Requires evidence of management commitment, customer focus, a quality policy, planning, definitions of responsibilities, proper authorities, internal communication, and management review. Note that as part of planning, the organization must define measurable objectives that are consistent with the quality policy.

- *Clause 6 (Resource management).* Requires provision of resources to implement the management system, continually improve its effectiveness, and enhance customer satisfaction. It also requires procedures to ensure competence of personnel, awareness of the importance of their activities, and a provision for training the organization's staff.

- *Clause 7 (Product and service realization).* Requires planning of the realization process, determination and review of customer requirements, and procedures for customer communication. There are subclauses defining the design-and-development process, including planning, inputs, outputs, review, verification, validation, and control of changes. There are also subclauses that require purchasing procedures, production and service provision, and the control of monitoring and measuring devices.

- *Clause 8 (Measurement, analysis, and improvement).* Contains subclauses for planning, monitoring, and measurement of customer satisfaction processes, products, and services. There are also subclauses that require documented procedures for internal audits, control of nonconforming products and services, and corrective and preventive action. Finally, there are subclauses requiring analysis of data and continual improvement of the management system. Note that the continual improvement process links back to management review in clause 5, which restarts the improvement cycle.

1.2.2 The documentation structure

The documentation structure can be pictured as a triangle with four sublevels, as shown in figure 1.1.

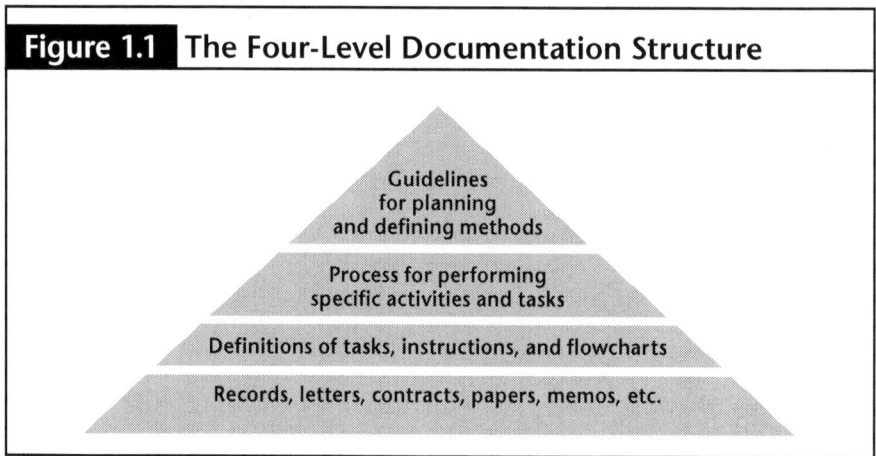

Figure 1.1   **The Four-Level Documentation Structure**

Guidelines
for planning
and defining methods

Process for performing
specific activities and tasks

Definitions of tasks, instructions, and flowcharts

Records, letters, contracts, papers, memos, etc.

The top level provides guidelines for planning and defining methods. The second level documents processes for performing specified activities and tasks. These documents describe inputs, outputs, customers, processes, interactions, and controls. The third level details how tasks are to be performed. The final level defines records that provide historical evidence that the policies, procedures, and work instructions are followed and that requirements have been achieved. A flowchart is an effective tool to document methods, tasks, and work instructions.

1.2.3 Lean Six Sigma: A project orientation

Lean and Six Sigma are usually linked operationally to improve process quality. Lean focuses on customer satisfaction and improved business performance and analyzes ways of reducing cycle time and waste. Anything that doesn't add value from the customer's perspective is defined as waste. Cycle time, operational costs, and customer and worker satisfaction are improved by eliminating waste.

Six Sigma reduces costs and increases profits by eliminating variability, defects, and waste. All work is a process and all processes have variability. Six Sigma focuses on customer satisfaction and improved business performance. Data gathered must be meaningful and related directly or indirectly to customer needs and expectations. Six Sigma uses tools such as design for Six Sigma (DFSS) and the define-measure-analyze-improve-control (DMAIC) methodology to improve processes. Six Sigma Black Belts and Green Belts are trained to identify and operate improvement projects.

1.2.4 Environmental management systems

Standardized EMS are usually based on ISO 14001,[4] which has environmental-specific requirements that are otherwise similar to those of ISO 9001. EMS protect against failure to satisfy governmental environmental care requirements. The following elements are part of an ISO 14001-compliant EMS:

■ Environmental policy
■ Planning:
  • Environmental aspects; legal and other requirements; and objectives, targets, and programs

■ Implementation and operation:
  • Resources, roles, responsibility, and authority; and competence, training, and awareness
  • Communication, control of documents, operational control, and emergency preparedness and response

■ Checking:
  • Monitoring and measurement, evaluation of compliance, and internal audits
  • Corrective and preventive actions and control of records

■ Management review

1.2.5 Information technology management systems

An effective IT system is very important to an organization's operations. Finance, sales, customer service and support, inventory management, enterprise resource planning (ERP), marketing, quality management, and human resources

---

4. *ISO 14001:2004, Environmental management systems—Requirements with guidance for use,* International Organization for Standardization (ISO), Geneva, Switzerland, 2004.

depend on an effective IT system. IT is also very important to SOX compliance, as proper data storage is critical to maintaining and analyzing data and protecting important corporate records.

IT has a major effect on how a QMS operates. It should also be noted that quality management has a major effect on the operation of the IT systems. Thus, the IT system is extremely important to the management of the data and processes of the QMS; likewise, the QMS provides tools for continual improvement of the IT system.

IT systems provide storage of records and documents, management and analysis of product data, services, personnel, customers, competitors, government requirements, research and development, and other topics. IT may also be used to control system transactions.

IT is an important factor in managing transactional systems such as supply chain management (SCM), ERP, and business continuity planning (BCP). SCM consists of planning, implementing, and controlling the operations of the supply chain. ERP is a process of monitoring and evaluating raw materials and reviewing related suppliers' quality and performance. BCP is a process used by an organization to create a plan for recovery and restoration of functions after an extended disruption of its facilities.

IT plays an important role in SOX compliance by directly supporting nine of its sections. This is especially true of the support needed to satisfy SOX section 404, which requires an effective system of internal control and the associated sets of supporting controls.

Finally, IT plays an important role in managing information security. The ISO/IEC 27000 series of standards describe the methodology and management system processes used to assure an effective system of information security, and the CobIT standard describes an effective tool for managing IT risk and controls.

1.2.6 Financial management system

A typical FMS consists of six elements: investment management, statement of cash flow, profit-and-loss statement (P&L), the balance sheet, the general ledger, and a system of internal control. We will look at each of these elements and how the other management systems can provide inputs and supports for financial management.

Investment management

The investment management process is where decisions about project costs and benefits are made. Some decision tools used are:

■ Payback on the original investment
■ Net present value (NPV) of the project: the cost of the investment discounted to reflect the time value of money.
■ Economic value added (EVA): the cost of the capital subtracted from its return value, multiplied by the amount of money invested.
■ Review of the variances associated with current budgets
■ Statistical forecasting to estimate the future results of investments
■ The break-even point, which occurs when total revenue received equals total costs associated with the sale of the product. Break-even analysis provides an understanding of profitability and is used to analyze the product mix.

QMS and EMS support of investment management focuses on strategic planning and management. Some examples of this support are supply chain management, new-product introduction, inventory management, marketing strategy, research-and-development management, customer communication, and intelligent management controls.

Cash flow statements

The cash flow statement describes day-to-day business operations. It reflects the flow of activity in the P&L statement and the balance sheet during day-to-day business operations (exclusive of investing and financing). There are three types of cash flows:

■ From operations
■ From investments
■ From financing

The following are common measures of cash flow:

■ Earnings before interest and taxes (EBIT) = operating revenue − operating expenses[5] + nonoperating income
■ EBITDA = EBIT + (depreciation and amortization)

---

5. Operating expenses include cost of goods sold, selling, general, and administration, depreciation; amortization; marketing; finance; human resources; administration; supply chain expenses; (transportation, distribution, warehousing, etc.); customer service; and other expenses.

- Net income = EBIT − (interest + taxes)
- Cash-burn ratio is the rate of negative cash flow per month.
- Variance analysis compares actual revenues and expenses with what was budgeted.

Figures 1.2 and 1.3 provide examples of typical elements found in cash flow statements and QMS/EMS support documents.

Figure 1.2 Sources of Funds

Sources of funds	QMS/EMS support
Net income	Improved focus on the customer, reduction in cost of operations
Accounts receivable	Effective product delivery and support
Bank notes	Strategic operations planning
Depreciation	Strategic product planning
Reduction in investments	Reduction in cost of operations, improved product performance

Figure 1.3 Use of Funds

Uses of funds	QMS/EMS support
Capital expenditures	Improved new product introduction, reduction in cost of production
Increased inventory	Quality management of inventory
Increased accounts payable	Effective supply chain management
Decreased long-term debt	Strategic planning
Payment of cash dividends	Reduced operating costs

The profit-and-loss statement

The P&L measures the performance of a business at a certain point in time and lists income and expenses. Income consists of revenues and earnings. Expenses include cost of goods sold (COGS); operating expenses; selling, general, and administrative (SG&A) expenses; depreciation; amortization; capital expense; income tax; and other expenses.

An important measure for stockholders is earnings per share. Net income is the difference between income and expenses and may be distributed as dividends to shareholders or held as retained earnings.

Managing an organization's quality and environmental processes helps provide information on its operating expenses. This includes SG&A expenses, sales and marketing, finance, human resources, administration, supply chain, and customer service. Other operating expenses include research and development (R&D), engineering, and the costs associated with running specific business units.

The following list describes how improvements to an organization's quality and environmental processes also improve its financial profile:

- Reduced operating and production costs
- Reduced transaction costs
- Reduced payroll
- Reduced cycle time
- Increased throughput (increased sales or revenue)
- Reduced supply costs
- Effective control of logistics
- Cost-effective management of inventories

Lean Six Sigma is a tool for reducing cost and improving quality. Lean increases efficiency, simplifies workflows, and eliminates waste. Six Sigma reduces variation, eliminates defects, and provides effective project management. Together, they improve an organization's bottom line.

The balance sheet

The balance sheet measures the financial health and liquidity of a business over time. Comparing the balance sheet at a sequence of times shows whether the value of the business is improving or declining. The balance sheet addresses the following:

- Current and long-term assets
- Liabilities:
  - Accounts payable
  - Taxes
  - Short-term debt

- Equity (total assets – total liabilities):
  - Common and preferred stock
  - Retained earnings

The following financial measures are associated with the balance sheet:

- P/E ratio = (market value per share)/(annual earnings per share)
- Market capitalization = (number of shares outstanding) × (price of shares)
- Asset turnover = revenue/total assets

- Return on investments (ROI) = profit/average investment
- Return on equity (ROE) = profit/average shareholder equity

Examples of how improvements to the quality and environmental processes also improve an organization's financials include:
- Shorter lead time and faster time to market
- Improved risk management
- Avoiding single-source suppliers
- Increased financial reliability
- Reduction in cash tied up in inventory
- Decreased spending of capital

Inventory management is a major part of quality management. The types of inventory under management consist of finished goods, work in progress, and raw materials. The major functions that quality management is responsible for are:
- First in-first out (FIFO) or last in-first out (LIFO) decisions
- Controlling inventory losses
- Estimating value
- Controlling turnover

The general ledger

The general ledger is where accounting transactions are recorded. It's the data source for most basic financial statements. The general ledger must always be in balance. Total assets must always equal total liabilities.

Assets consist of the following: current assets, fixed assets, depreciation, investments, and inventory. Current assets include cash and income from the sale of goods and services and accounts receivable. Fixed assets are land, buildings, machinery and equipment, vehicles, patents, trademarks, and copyrights. Depreciation is used to allocate tangible assets purchased over their useful life. Investments mainly consist of ownership or equity in other companies.

Liabilities include debt, stockholder equity, accounts payable, payroll and benefits, operating expenses, COGS, and other obligations.

Much of the data in the general ledger are provided by quality and environmental management. This includes results from Lean Six Sigma projects.

The system of internal control

An effective system of internal control is required by clause 404 of SOX. Internal control[6] is a process controlled by an entity's board of directors, management, and other personnel designed to provide reasonable assurance regarding the achievement of objectives in the following categories:[7]

- Effectiveness and efficiencies of operations
- Reliability of financial reporting
- Compliance with applicable laws and regulations

SOX requires that third-party auditors obtain assurance from the organization's CEO and CFO that their system is effective. The result should be increased transparency in the organization.

Chapter 2 includes a discussion of the requirements for internal control and how ISO 9001 and ISO 14001 can provide support for a compliant system.

1.3 QMS AND EMS SUPPORT OF FINANCIAL MANAGEMENT[8]

Quality improvements contribute to financial management in a number of ways. First of all, hard savings affect the P&L statement and increased income from the sales of high-quality products affects the bottom line.

Soft savings are more difficult to quantify, but they affect the balance sheet. For example, reduction in cash tied up in inventory or the avoidance of planned capacity enhancements results in decreased spending of capital. Very soft savings include improved customer and employee satisfaction and increased safety in workplace.

EMS provide an understanding of significant aspects of environmental and related legal requirements and the means of satisfying them. Environmental problems can be very costly to an organization and can take large amounts of resources to correct.

Finally, two supporting technologies play important roles in an organization. Without an effective IT system, the financial, quality, and environmental manage-

---

6. Internal Control—Integrated Framework, Committee of Sponsoring Organizations of the Treadway Commission (COSO). Published by COSO, September 1992 and May 1994.
7. Ibid.
8. For ISO 9001 and ISO 14001 support of COSO guidance see: Sandford Liebesman, "Mitigate SOX Risk with ISO 9001 and 14001," *Quality Progress*, September 2005, 91–93.

ment systems will have difficulty operating. Lean Six Sigma projects provide bottom-line improvements that directly affect the financial results of the organization.

1.3.1 Benefits of QMS and EMS support

Financial managers will gain a better understanding of current operations when they understand the role of QMS and EMS. The result is a much more accurate measure of the status and effectiveness of the organization. Also, QMS/EMS support will lead to greater transparency. QMS/EMS are essential to the practice of continual improvement.

The support of QMS/EMS will help top management and the board of directors identify business risks, control them, and prevent major surprises. These management systems provide added resources (especially for internal auditing). They help reduce the cost of compliance and improve corporate governance by connecting management systems.

One benefit of connecting an organization's management systems is the consistent set of procedures this approach produces. ISO 9001 requires six documented procedures that can also be used by other management systems:

- Control of documents (clause 4.2.3)
- Control of records (clause 4.2.4)
- Internal auditing (clause 8.2.2)
- Control of nonconforming product (clause 8.3)
- Corrective action (clause 8.5.2)
- Preventive action (clause 8.5.3)

1.4 OUTLINE OF THE REST OF THE BOOK

SOX requirements are introduced in chapter 2 with a discussion of specific elements of SOX. Next is a discussion on how ISO 9001 and ISO 14001 support compliance to SOX clause 404, which requires an effective system of internal control. This is done by comparing these standards to the five Committee of Sponsoring Organizations (COSO) elements.

A risk management methodology is defined in chapter 3, which includes key tools for managing and mitigating risks. The risk management process consists of defining the organization's objectives, specifying the risk categories, identifying risks to the objectives, and developing methods for managing these risks.

The role of IT is discussed in chapter 4. An effective IT system is a necessity in the operation of any business, and multiple software applications are needed. Chapter 4 also describes the effect IT has on SOX, specific internal controls, and information security.

Chapter 5 describes how Lean Six Sigma links to financial management, ISO 9001, ISO 14001, and IT. Included is a discussion of various types of waste and the tools used to understand and reduce them. The discussion of Six Sigma includes a description of the define-measure-analyze-improve-control (DMAIC) and define-measure-analyze-design-validate (DMADV) methodologies.

Chapter 6 focuses on the structure of a linked management system and indicates what management must do to assure its effectiveness. The methodology for implementing a linked management system consists of four phases: planning, development, internal assessment, and external auditing. The description includes deliverables for each phase.

Chapter 7 includes a set of case studies of organizations that linked their management systems to comply with SOX clause 404. Two questionnaires are used to understand how these organizations accomplished this. It also includes a linked management system story that illustrates how an organization improved communication between quality and financial auditors. Chapter 7 also contains examples of case studies from a new ISO book that provides guidance on how to integrate requirements of multiple ISO and non-ISO management system standards.

Chapter 8 describes an eight-step philosophy that organizations should consider as they start the development of their management systems linking program. A key point made is that members of the management systems lack the ability to communicate with each other. The chapter ends with an elevator speech that describes how linking the management systems can improve the bottom line.

Chapter 2

QMS/EMS Support of the Sarbanes-Oxley Act

2.1 THE SARBANES-OXLEY ACT OF 2002

The Sarbanes-Oxley Act (SOX) was published in 2002 in response to financial scandals at Enron, WorldCom, and other companies that misused corporate resources. The act created the Public Company Accounting Oversight Board (PCAOB) under the Securities and Exchange Commission (SEC). The SEC enforces SOX and oversees the PCAOB. SOX requires management to assess the effectiveness of the internal control system and procedures and mandates CEOs and CFOs to personally certify their financial statements and disclosures. SOX also requires internal control monitoring, records management, and whistleblower protection.

SOX is the latest in a series of financial market regulations that started with the crash of financial markets in 1929. The first of these regulations were the Securities Act of 1933 and the Securities Exchange Act of 1934. From the 1930s through the 1970s, the Financial Accounting Standards Board (FASB) developed the Generally Accepted Accounting Principles (GAAP).[1] In the 1970s more than 400 companies made illegal payments to government personnel, which led to the development of the Foreign Corrupt Practices Act of 1977. This resulted in the establishment of internal accounting controls.

In the 1980s, insider trading scandals led to the creation of the Treadway Commission, which consisted of five major accounting professional societies. The commission developed the Committee of Sponsoring Organizations (COSO) guidance[2]

---

1. Edward Fields, *The Essentials of Finance and Accounting for Nonfinancial Managers* (American Management Association, 2002).
2. *Internal Control—Integrated Framework*, Committee of Sponsoring Organizations of the Treadway Commission (COSO). Published by COSO, September 1992 and May 1994.

for management of internal control systems. However, because the laws didn't require an effective system of internal control, COSO was generally ignored.

On December 2, 2001, Enron filed for bankruptcy with $63.4 billion in assets. This was followed by WorldCom, whose $107 billion bankruptcy made it the largest bankruptcy in history, and then HealthSouth, Tyco, and Adelphia. Investors lost billions. This included middle-class employees who kept their retirement accounts in company stocks. Other companies followed, leading to the 2002 stock market sell-off.

SOX's major goal was improving the transparency of a corporation's financial statements by requiring public companies to have an effective system of internal control. The key SOX principles are independence, accountability, transparency, deterrence, accuracy, and responsibility.

Any company that lists its securities in the United States has to comply with SOX. This includes large companies (accelerated filers), mid-size companies (accelerated filers), and small companies (nonaccelerated filers).

2.1.1 THE STRUCTURE OF SOX

SOX consists of eleven major sections. The emphasis in the media is on compliance to section 404 because of the large costs to comply with it and the penalties for failure. But there are many other risks, and we will review them.

Figure 2.1   Eleven Titles of SOX

Title	Section
Title I: Public Company Accounting Oversight	101–109
Title II: Auditor Independence	201–209
Title III: Corporate Responsibility	301–308
Title IV: Enhanced Financial Disclosures	401–409
Title V: Analyst Conflicts of Interest	501
Title VI: Commission Resources and Authority	601–604
Title VII: Studies and Reports	701–705
Title VIII: Corporate and Criminal Fraud Accountability	801–807
Title IX: White-Collar Crime Penalty Enhancement	901–906
Title X: Corporate Tax Returns	1001
Title XI: Corporate Fraud and Accountability	1101–1107

Figure 2.1 lists the eleven sections of SOX. Each section has multiple subsections. Only the key subsections will be described below. See appendix A for a complete listing of the SOX sections.

Title I: Public Company Accounting Oversight

Under title 1, section 103 of the PCAOB was established as part of the SEC. The PCAOB registers public accounting firms, inspects them, investigates issues with respect to them, runs disciplinary proceedings, and provides sanctions when necessary. The PCAOB also enforces SOX compliance and adopts audit standards to implement the internal controls required by section 404. Its revised audit standard No. 5 was approved in July 2007.[3] On August 15, 2010, the PCAOB approved auditing standards No. 8 through 15 covering the auditor's assessment of and response to risk.

On June 25, 2007, the SEC published "Guidance Regarding Management's Report on Internal Control Over Financial Reporting."[4] Note that public accounting firms must maintain working papers for at least seven years. Recently, COSO developed a guidance document for enterprise risk management that expands its criteria.[5]

Title II: Auditor Independence

External auditors cannot perform internal audit functions, install financial systems, or provide financial statements or bookkeeping services for its clients. Also, they cannot move their personnel into the client's corporate positions or provide investment or auditing legal services.

Title III: Corporate Responsibility

Section 302 covers quarterly and annual financial reproduction. It puts responsibility squarely on the CEO and CFO to certify the appropriateness of financial statements and disclosures, identify material weakness or significant changes in the organization's internal controls, and correct significant deficiencies and material weaknesses. Note that ISO 9001 and ISO 14001 provide corrective and preven-

---

3. The ASQ SOX team provided inputs to the revised Audit Standard Number 5 and the SEC Guidance. See the article that appeared in *Quality Progress*: Sandford Liebesman, "ASQ Team Says QMS and EMS Standards."
4. Ibid.
5 "Enterprise Risk Management—Integrated Framework; Executive Summary Framework," American Institute of Certified Public Accountants, Jersey City, NJ, 2004.

tive action procedures. These can provide early indications of problem areas. SOX requires organizations to correct significant deficiencies and material weaknesses before third-party auditors can sign off on the audit.

Title IV: Enhanced Financial Disclosures

Section 404 requires management to document its assessment of the effectiveness of internal controls. External auditors must attest to and report on assessments made by management. They can't sign off if there is a significant deficiency or material weakness. Before managers can attest to the effectiveness of the controls, they have to ensure that they can recognize problems, analyze their severity, and understand and communicate their materiality. Revenue recognition is generally recognized as a problem. This is often due to the misuse of spreadsheets.[6]

Section 409 covers real-time disclosures. The organization must immediately communicate to the public changes that could affect investment and purchasing decisions and must disclose material changes on a rapid and current basis. This is aimed at reducing the need to restate financial results. Quality management systems (QMS) and environmental management systems (EMS) can help with compliance to this section by identifying risks in real time.

Title VIII: Corporate and Criminal Fraud Accountability

Section 802 covers criminal penalties for altering documents. The organization cannot destroy, alter, or falsify records in a federal investigation or bankruptcy hearing. Personnel who do are subject to fines and up to twenty years in prison. Accountants must maintain their audit work papers for five years. If they don't, members of the organization are subject to fines and up to ten years in prison. The information technology (IT) department has a major role in complying with section 802. ISO/IEC 27001[7] is a new tool that can be used to assure security of information.

Section 806 provides for protection of whistleblower. Management may not discharge, demote, suspend, threaten, harass, or in any other manner discriminate against a whistleblower. Organizations must have a way to protect a whistleblower's identity. Compensatory damages may include reinstatement with same seniority status, back pay with interest, and special damages.

---

6. See *www.revenuerecognition.com*.
7. ISO/IEC 27001:2005, Information technology—Security techniques—Specification for an information security management system, International Organization for Standardization, Geneva, Switzerland, 2005.

Section 807 defines criminal penalties for defrauding shareholders. This section protects shareholders from fraud in connection with any security of an issuer. It's illegal to obtain representations or promises of money or property in connection with the purchase or sale of securities by false or fraudulent pretenses. Criminal penalties include fines and/or twenty-five years in prison.

Title IX: White-Collar Crime Penalty Enhancement

Section 906 describes requirements for certifying periodic reports. The CEO and CFO must make statements certifying compliance with the Securities Exchange Act of 1934. The report must fairly present the organization's financial condition. Criminal penalties in this section are up to $5 million and imprisonment for up to twenty years. If there is no intent to misrepresent, the penalties are up to $1 million and up to ten years in prison.

Title XI: Corporate Fraud and Accountability

Section 1102 covers tampering with a record or otherwise impeding an official proceeding. It is illegal to alter, destroy, mutilate, or conceal a record, document, or other like objects. It is also illegal to obstruct, influence, or impede official proceedings. The penalty consists of fines and imprisonment for up to twenty years. IT personnel have a major role in complying with the requirements in section 1102.

Figure 2.2 contains a summary of the risks and penalties in SOX.

2.2 A SYSTEM OF INTERNAL CONTROL

COSO defines internal control[8] as a process, affected by an entity's board of directors, management, and other personnel, that's designed to provide reasonable assurance regarding the achievement of objectives in the following categories:

■ Effectiveness and efficiencies of operations
■ Reliability of financial reporting
■ Compliance with applicable laws and regulations

Internal control is based on the following fundamental concepts:

■ Internal control is a process.
■ Internal control is affected by people.

---

8. *Internal Control—Integrated Framework*, Committee of Sponsoring Organizations of the Treadway Commission (COSO) Published by COSO, September 1992 and May 1994.

Figure 2.2 Risks and Penalties in SOX

Section	Risk	Penalties
302, 404	Certify financial statements and disclosures.	See section 906.
		Fines up to $5 million and/or jail up to twenty years. If there is no intent to misrepresent, fines up to $1 million and jail up to ten years.
302, 404	Identify and correct significant deficiencies and material weaknesses.	See section 906.
409	Disclose material changes on a rapid and current basis.	None
802	Destruction, alteration, or falsification of corporate records	Fines and/or jail up to twenty years
	Destruction of corporate audit records	Fines and or jail up to ten years
806, 1107	Suits from whistleblower	Fine and/or jail up to ten years
807	Securities fraud	Fines and/or jail up to twenty-five years
906	Incorrect or false certification of the organization's financial condition	Fines up to $5 million and/or jail up to twenty years. If there is no intent to misrepresent, fines up to $1 million and jail up to ten years.
1102	Alter, destroy, mutilate, or conceal a record, document, or other object	Fines and/or jail up to twenty years
1102	Obstruct, influence, or impede official proceedings	Fines and/or jail up to twenty years

■ Internal control can be expected to provide reasonable assurance, not absolute assurance.

■ Internal control is geared to achievement of objectives.

The purposes of internal control are to aid in achieving an organization's goals and objectives, assist in reliable financial reporting and compliance, lead the organization through its day-to-day operations, and provide rules or guidelines for activities that identify and mitigate risks. Note that a system of internal control is there for guidance, but it won't ensure success or achievement of business goals.

Internal control must be established, maintained, analyzed, and assessed for effectiveness, and the CEO and CFO must certify that the internal controls are sufficient and have been monitored within ninety days of filing the report.

The audit of internal control is a report attesting to the effectiveness of the internal control system, and it is required each fiscal year. It must describe material changes in the internal control system. A report must be completed every quarter addressing the design and effectiveness of the system and must provide proof of actual tests of the controls and the results of those tests. Note that a "negative assurance" or a statement that "nothing has come to management's attention" is not sufficient.

2.3 DEVELOPING AN INTERNAL CONTROL SYSTEM FOR SOX

The following steps are recommended to develop an effective system of internal control:

1. Establish a compliance committee.
2. Design a COSO-based system.
3. Prepare a formal implementation plan.
4. Assess risk.
5. Set reporting objectives.
6. Communicate the procedures.
7. Provide training.
8. Document processes and risk management.
9. Perform continuous evaluations, including internal audits.

The SEC suggests testing the following controls:

■ Initiating, recording, processing, and reconciling account balances
■ Classes of transactions and disclosure-related assertions
■ Processing of nonroutine transactions
■ Selection/application of accounting policies
■ Prevention, identification, and detection of fraud

Some specific examples of controls to test are separation of duties requiring more than one signature on checks, policies to assure password control, consistent reconciliation procedures, well-defined ethics policies, and competence training.

One method of assessing the reliability of the internal control system is to review the extent of documentation of the processes and controls, determine the awareness of system within the organization, monitor and evaluate the results of the controls, and evaluate the design and operating effectiveness of the system.

2.4 COSO AND SOX 404

COSO published *Internal Control—Integrated Framework* in 1992 and *COSO Evaluation Tools* in 1994. The SEC recommends using the COSO guidance for SOX 404 compliance.

The integrated framework consists of the three objectives and five elements depicted in figure 2.3. A compliant system of internal control assures achievement of COSO'S objectives:

■ Effectiveness and efficiency of operations
■ Reliability of financial reporting
■ Compliance with laws and regulations

Figure 2.3 **The COSO Elements of Internal Control[9]**

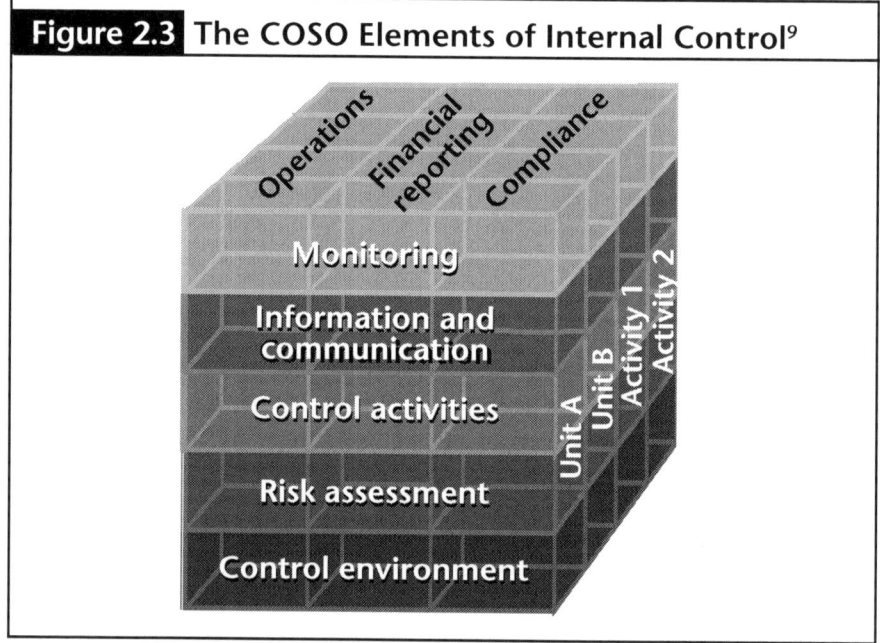

---

9. *Internal Control—Integrated Framework.* Committee of Sponsoring Organizations of the Treadway Commission (COSO), September 1992 and May 1994.

The controls must be preventive and corrective and provide a mechanism for managing risk. Note that ISO 9001 and ISO 14001 require preventive and corrective action support for a compliant system of internal control.

COSO consists of five interrelated components. These are derived from the way management runs the business and are integrated with the management process. Although the components apply to all entities, small and mid-size companies may implement them differently than large ones. Their controls may be less formal and less structured, yet a small company can still have an effective internal control process. The components are:

■ Control environment
■ Information and communication
■ Risk assessment
■ Monitoring
■ Control activities

2.5 ISO 9001 AND ISO 14001 SUPPORT OF COSO

The COSO control environment element is the foundation for all other COSO elements providing discipline and structure. In a typical organization, there are hard controls and soft controls. Hard controls consist of the organization's structure, operational controls, reporting levels, human resources policies, and board of directors involvement. Effective hard controls should answer the question: "Does the organization do things *right*?" Soft controls consist of the ethics practiced in the organization, competence of personnel, and style of management. Effective soft controls should answer a second question: "Does the organization do the right *things*?"

In an effective control environment, management must maintain a high degree of integrity in its dealings and require its employees and agents to maintain similar levels of integrity. Departures from this requirement should be dealt with quickly and severely. There should be examples on file of actions taken with respect to individuals and with regard to general communication. Few complaints alleging misconduct should be received from customers or others.

ISO 9001's support of a control environment is demonstrated by the following:
■ The process approach, addressed in clause 4.1, defines the basic structure of the organization's processes and how the organization operates. Clause 6.1 requires provision of resources needed to meet customer requirements.

- Clause 5.1 requires evidence of management commitment.
- Clauses 7.1 and 8.1 require planning of the product realization and measurement, analysis, and improvement activities.
- Clauses 5.3, 5.4.1, 5.5.3, and 6.2.2 contain requirements for a quality policy, measurable objectives, internal communication, and employee competence.

The process approach as defined in clause 4.1 requires identification of all processes and their application; determination of their sequence and interaction; definition of criteria and methods to assure that processes are effective; provision of resources and information to support operation and monitoring of the processes; monitoring, measuring, and analyzing the processes; and implementing actions to achieve results and continual improvement.

COSO's information and communication element requires that pertinent information be identified, captured, and communicated in a form and time frame that enables people to perform their responsibilities. Information systems produce reports containing operational, financial, and compliance-related information that makes it possible to operate and control the business. They deal not only with internally generated data, but also with information about external events, activities, and conditions necessary to make informed business decisions.

Some questions related to information and communication are:

- How is information identified, captured, and communicated?
- Does information flow up, across, and down the organization?
- Do employees understand their roles in control processes?
- Are processes in place to address employee, supplier, and customer concerns in a timely manner?

ISO 9001's support of information and communication starts with control of documents, which is addressed in clause 4.2.3, and control of records, which is addressed in clause 4.2.4. ISO 9001 requires a documented procedure to control approval, review, update, identification, and the use of current revisions of documents to ensure legibility of documents in use, control of external documents, and removal of obsolete documents from use. For control of records a documented procedure is required to control the identification, storage, protection, retrieval, retention time, and disposal of records.

Communication requirements are defined for three stakeholders: the organization, its customers, and its suppliers. For internal communication, clauses 5.1 and 5.5.3 require that top management make a clear commitment to the importance of meeting customer, statutory, and regulatory requirements. For customer communication, clause 7.2 requires determination and review of customer requirements; clause 7.2.3 requires direct communication with customers on product information, customer enquiries, and customer feedback.

Clause 7.4 requires supplier communication through the purchasing process. In clause 7.4.2, the supplier must be provided with information concerning product and service management requirements, supplier personnel qualification, and verification procedures for purchased products.

COSO's risk assessment element is the identification and analysis of relevant risks to the achievement of objectives and the basis for determining how risks should be managed. A precondition to risk assessment is establishment of objectives that are linked at different levels and internally consistent. Because economic, industry, regulatory, and operating conditions will change, mechanisms are needed to deal with change and the resulting risks.

Risk assessment and management includes identification and analysis of risks that may prevent achieving objectives. Effective risk assessment requires:

- Definition of the objectives
- Determination of the compatibility of the objectives
- Identification of risks to achieving the objectives
- Judgment as to which risks are critical
- Determination of actions to mitigate risks starting with critical actions
- A mechanism for dealing with change

ISO 9001's support of risk assessment starts with the development of measurable objectives in clause 5.4.1. These objectives are the major determining factors for risk assessment. Next, the organization needs to review the customer requirements for high-risk elements that can affect its ability to serve the customer. This is accomplished in clause 7.2, which describes the contract review process. ISO 9001 also requires the organization to monitor and measure its processes and products in clauses 8.2.3 and 8.2.4 and provide this data for analysis in clause 8.4. Other inputs to clause 8.4 are customer satisfaction data from clause 8.2.1, supplier data from clause 7.4.3, and internal audit results from clause 8.2.2.

The goal of clause 8.4 is to turn the data into information that can be used to identify risks to the organization. This clause requires analysis of trends in the data, which provides early identification of risks. The trends are used to identify opportunities for corrective and preventive action using the documented procedures required by clauses 8.5.2 and 8.5.3. Finally, the information obtained using clause 8.4 and the progress of the corrective and preventive actions are inputs to the continual improvement clause (8.5.1) and the management review process defined in clause 5.6.

ISO 14001:2004's support of risk assessment consists of requirements similar to those of ISO 9001 with additional tools to reduce environmental risk. The requirements similar to ISO 9001:2008 include defining measurable objectives and targets, monitoring and measuring environmental performance, evaluating compliance, and management review. ISO 14001's clause 4.3.1 defines environmental aspects as "elements of an organization's activities, products or services which can interact with the environment." As an added requirement this clause requires the organization to identify its significant aspects. These aspects form the basis for identifying environmental risks.

COSO's monitoring element requires a process that assesses the quality of the system's performance over time. This is accomplished through separate evaluations, ongoing monitoring activities, or a combination of the two. A key tool used by organizations is internal auditing. Ongoing monitoring occurs in the course of operations. It includes regular management, supervisory activities, and other actions personnel take in performing their duties. Internal control should be monitored to determine adequate design, proper execution, and effectiveness. The audit committee should annually review the monitoring program to assure coverage of high-risk elements.

Management is responsible for determining how best to implement adequate monitoring and enforcement mechanisms. The chief accounting officer is responsible for monitoring the company's financial reporting system and internal accounting controls. The internal audit function is an important element in preventing and detecting fraudulent financial reporting. The internal audit group must have a pulse on the control system. Auditors must be able to drill down to root causes and be effective in following audit trails. Two major concerns for internal auditors are to identify significant deficiencies and material weaknesses, which must be identified and corrected before third-party audits. See appendix C for a definition of significant deficiencies and material weaknesses. These need to be identified before the external auditors arrive.

ISO 9001 and ISO 14001's support of monitoring is closely related to their support of risk assessment. This includes ISO 9001's clauses that describe measurable objectives (clause 5.4.1); monitoring and measurement of processes (clause 8.2.3), products (clause 8.2.4), and data analysis (clause 8.4). In addition, there are requirements for internal auditing (clause 8.2.2), measuring customer satisfaction (clause 8.2.1), and continual improvement (clause 8.5.1). These requirements provide inputs to management review (clause 5.6). ISO 14001 has similar clauses that address monitoring and measurement (4.5.1), evaluation of compliance (4.5.2), internal audit (4.5.5), management review (4.6), and continual improvement (4.6.2).

COSO's **control activities element** consists of the policies and procedures that help ensure management directives are followed. These include approvals, verifications, asset security, authorizations, reconciliations, and the segregation of duties. Control activities help ensure that necessary actions are taken to address risks to the achievement of the entity's objectives and that appropriate and timely action is taken on exceptions, risks, or information that requires follow-up.

The company's process for identifying control activities is based on its objectives and risks and what appears to be effective. Special control activities are put in place for significant plans and programs. For example, actions needed for inbound activities, such as management of supplier products or outsourced services.

ISO 9001 and ISO 14001's support of control activities is centered on the management review processes in each standard. These are described in clause 5.6 of ISO 9001 and clause 4.6 of ISO 14001. ISO 9001 also requires documented procedures for control of nonconforming product (clause 8.3), corrective action (clause 8.5.2), and preventive action (clause 8.5.3). ISO 14001 has similar requirements for nonconformities and corrective and preventive actions (clause 4.5.3) and emergency preparedness and responses (clauses 4.4.7).

Figure 2.4 is a summary of the support ISO 9001 and ISO 14001 provide for the five elements of the COSO guidance.

Figure 2.4 ISO 9001 and ISO 14001 Support of COSO

COSO Model for SOX	ISO 9001	Clause
1. Internal control environment ■ Foundation for all other COSO elements ■ Does the organization do things right? ■ Does the organization do the right things and maintain a high degree of integrity in its dealings? ■ Few complaints alleging misconduct are received from customers or others. ■ Competence of personnel maintained. ■ Effective management style or "tone at the top" maintained.	4.1	Quality management system: General requirements
	5.1	Management commitment
	5.3	Quality policy
	5.4.1	Quality objectives
	5.5.3	Internal communication
	6.1	Provision of resources
	6.2.2	Competence, training, and awareness
	7.1	Planning of product realization
	8.1	Planning of measurement, analysis, and improvement
	ISO 14001 clauses 4.4.1, 4.4.7, and 4.4.6	■ Resources, roles, responsibilities, and authority (ISO 14001 clause 4.4.1) ■ Emergency preparedness and response (ISO 14001 clause 4.4.7) ■ Operational control (ISO 14001 clause 4.4.6)
2. Information and communication ■ Information captured and communicated enabling people to perform their responsibilities. ■ Reports used to run and control the business ■ Information about external events, activities, and conditions for making informed business decisions ■ How is information identified, captured, and communicated? ■ Does it flow across the organization? ■ Do employees understand their roles in the control process? ■ Are there processes in place to address employee, supplier, and customer concerns in a timely manner?	4.2.3	Control of documents
	4.2.4	Control of records
	5.1a	Internal commitment
	5.5.3	Internal communication
	6.2.2	Competence, awareness, and training
	7.2.1	Determine of requirements related to the product
	7.2.3	Customer communication
	7.4	Purchasing
	8.4	Analysis of data

Figure 2.4 ISO 9001 and ISO 14001 Support of COSO (cont.)

COSO Model for SOX	ISO 9001	Clause
3. Risk assessment ■ Establishment of objectives, linked at different levels and internally consistent ■ Identification, analysis, and management of risks to achieving objectives ■ Mechanisms to deal with change and the risks relevant to change ■ Effective risk assessment requires: • Definition of the objectives • Determination of the compatibility of the objectives • Identification of risks to achieving the objectives • Determination of risks associated with changes • Judgment as to which risks are critical • Determination of actions to mitigate risks starting with the critical ones	4.1 (last paragraph)	Control of outsourced processes
	5.4.1	Quality objectives
	5.6	Management review
	6.3	Infrastructure
	7.2	Customer-related processes
	7.4	Purchasing
	8.2	Monitoring and measurement
	8.4	Analysis of data
	8.5	Improvement
	ISO 14001 clauses 4.3.1 and 4.5.2	■ Environmental aspects and identification of significant aspects (ISO 14001 clause 4.3.1) ■ Evaluation of compliance (ISO 14001 clause 4.5.2)
4. Monitoring ■ A process that assesses the quality of the system's performance over time through separate evaluations and/or ongoing monitoring activities ■ Key tools include internal auditing, management, and supervision of operations and actions of personnel performing their duties. ■ Management is responsible for implementation. ■ Auditors must drill down to root causes, follow audit trails, and identify significant deficiencies and material weaknesses.	4.2.3	Control of documents
	4.2.4	Control of records
	5.4.1	Quality objectives
	5.6	Management review
	6.2.2	Competence, awareness, and training
	7.2	Customer-related processes
	8.2.	Monitoring and measurement
	8.4	Analysis of data
	8.5	Improvement

| Figure 2.4 | ISO 9001 and ISO 14001 Support of COSO (cont.) | |

COSO Model for SOX	ISO 9001	Clause
5. Control activities	4.1c	Effective processes
■ Policies and procedures that help ensure management directives are followed, including approvals, verifications, the security of assets, authorizations, reconciliations, and the segregation of duties.	ISO 9001 clause 5.6 and ISO 14001 clause 4.6	Management review
	6.3	Infrastructure
■ Timely actions taken to address risks to the achievement of the entity's objectives, exceptions, and information that requires follow-up.	7.4.3	Verification of purchased products
	8.3	Control of nonconforming product
■ Control activities are based on objectives, risks, and what appears to be effective.	8.5	Improvement
	ISO 14001 clause 4.4.7	Emergency preparedness and response
■ Control activities are put in place for significant plans and programs, such as the management of supplier products and outsourced services.	ISO 14001 clause 4.5.3	Nonconformity, corrective action, and preventive action

2.6 BENEFITS OF QMS AND EMS SUPPORT OF INTERNAL CONTROLS

Financial management will gain a better understanding of current operations when the organization's QMS and EMS support its internal controls. The result is a much more accurate measure of the status and effectiveness of the organization. QMS and EMS support will lead to greater transparency and continual improvement.

The support of QMS/EMS will help top management and the board of directors identify business risks, control them, and prevent major surprises. These management systems provide added resources (especially for internal auditing), help reduce the cost of compliance, and improve corporate governance by connecting management systems.

2.7 CHAPTER 2 EXERCISES: SOX RISK

Identify the likelihood of each of the following SOX risks and the areas of the organizations most likely to contribute to it.

Table 2.1	SOX Risks		
Section	**Risk**	**Likelihood (H, M, L)***	**Major contributor(s)**
302	Certify financial statements and disclosures.		
302	Identify and correct significant deficiencies and material weaknesses.		
409	Disclose material changes on a rapid and current basis.		
802	Destruction, alteration, or falsification of corporate records		
806	Suits from whistleblowers		
807	Securities fraud		
906	Incorrect certification of the organization's financial condition		
1102	Alter, destroy, mutilate, or conceal a record, document, or other object		
1102	Obstruct, influence, or impede official proceedings		

(H, M, L) = High, Medium, Low

Chapter 3

Risk Management's Importance in Today's Economy

3.1 INTRODUCTION

The global economy has provided organizations with many opportunities that didn't exist even ten years ago. It also presents many risks because of the flattening of the Earth via the Internet and extensive outsourcing to countries such as China and Mexico. The designers of the Committee of Sponsoring Organizations of the Treadway Commission (COSO) guidance commonly used for Sarbanes-Oxley (SOX) compliance recognized the importance of risk by including risk assessment as one element of its system of internal control.

The Treadway Commission has also developed an enterprise risk management process[1] that includes not just risks associated with accidental losses, but also financial, strategic, operational, and other risks. Risk is defined as the expected cost of failures. It's the product of the probability of occurrence and the cost of failure.

All organizations are continually subjected to many risks. The importance of each risk is defined by its effect on the objectives of the organization. By linking the management systems, each system's tools help manage risk in the other systems and across the entire organization.

The starting point is an understanding of the organization's objectives and the identification of the common risks of these objectives. Risks appear at many levels

---

1. The Committee of Sponsoring Organizations of the Treadway Commission, "Enterprise Risk Management—Integrated Framework; Executive Summary Framework." (American Institute of Certified Public Accountants, 2004).

within the organization and at various levels of concern for management. Risk controls should be prioritized using a top-down, risk-based approach.

3.2 TYPES OF RISK

Organizations must consider four types of risk: strategic, organizational, compliance, and operational.

3.2.1 Strategic risk

Strategic risk occurs when the organization chooses a strategy that reflects an inappropriate alignment between the organization and its external environment. It's concerned with the inability to achieve high-level goals.

For strategic risk assessment, management should consider technology changes, creditors' demands, competitors' actions, economic conditions, political conditions, and customer needs. These are considerations that should be included in the quality management system (QMS) planning process described in ISO 9001:2008, clause 5.4.2.

3.2.2 Organizational risk

Organizational risk is based on an organization's structure and is found on two levels: the entity level and the activity level. Entity-level risks are either external or internal and affect the entire organization. External factors affecting organizational risks include technology developments, competition, and new legislation. Internal risk factors are physical security, information system processing, lost shipping and receiving records, personnel competence, and changes in management responsibilities.

Activity-level risks affect individual units or functions in the organization. Risks observed at the activity level include not entering information or materials received into the system on a timely basis, lost receiving reports or shipping records, poor physical security control, inadequate skilled labor, and employee carelessness. Activity-level risks occur across the organization, and they will affect entity-level risks.

3.2.3 Compliance risk

Compliance risk affects an organization's ability to comply with legal and regulatory requirements. The focus is on financial, environmental, health and safety, and security factors. Government-mandated environmental and health and safety requirements cause concern because of the risk of fines, shutdowns, or criminal prosecution for noncompliance. There is also a concern with conformance to quality and environmental standards and specifications.

Environmental risks include liquid spills, gaseous emissions, and solid waste. ISO 14001 requires monitoring and measurement of environmental risks, identification of significant environmental aspects, and evaluation of compliance to the standard.

Some examples of environmental risks are:

- Purchasing department shifts from a domestic to a foreign chemical supplier
- Downsizing results in a key environmental manager not being replaced
- A material specification change requires a new material safety data sheet that hasn't been developed
- ISO 14001 not on top management's radar screen

The Environmental Protection Agency (EPA) has recognized the value of ISO 14001 in managing risk by establishing the National Environmental Performance Track[2], which provides incentives for participation, including lower priority for routine EPA inspections and use of the program's logo. An important part of the program's members' leadership role in environmental performance is their commitment to continued compliance. This commitment is evidenced by implementation of an environmental management system (EMS) that requires a commitment to compliance, periodic EMS and compliance audits, and an annual certification of compliance.

3.2.4 Operational risk

Operational risk concentrates on factors that may prevent the efficient use of resources. This risk is where the majority of the staff effort occurs in an organization.

Operational risk consists of seven categories: management system, customer satisfaction, supply chain, revenue recognition, information security, logistics, and natural disasters.

3.2.5 The risk of ineffective management systems

A management system may be ineffective due to its strategies, practices and tools, data processing, call centers, contract administration, and design and development. There are a number of specific risks faced by top management. First of all, there is the risk of a highly outsourced supply chain. Some companies outsource

---

2. *www.epa.gov/PerformanceTrack*

60 to 80 percent of their products. Unfortunately, most managers don't have the technical background to understand what is going on in their suppliers' organizations.

Other management system risks include revenue recognition; the effects of homeland security; government-mandated environmental requirements that may result in fines, shutdowns, or criminal prosecution; and the risk of not satisfying SOX. Compliance to ISO 9001 can be used to improve responses to these risks.

The following activities can adversely affect a management system:

- Poor management
- Poor human resources management
- Lack of effective management tools
- Data-processing errors
- Ineffective call centers
- Poor marketing strategies
- Poor contract administration
- Customer communication issues
- Design-and-development problems

Top management and the board of directors need to understand their management systems and coordinate efforts to improve effectiveness.

3.2.6 Customer satisfaction risk

Customer satisfaction risk is affected by customer communication, delivery problems, product quality, design problems, repair problems, and the accuracy of customer feedback. ISO 9001:2008 requires gathering and analyzing customer satisfaction data regarding whether the organization has met the customer's requirements (clause 8.2.1). These data are input into a process of analysis (clause 8.4) along with product quality data, product and process monitoring data, and inputs on supplier quality.

The main output of clause 8.4 is a transformation of the data into information that can be used for continual improvement (clause 8.5.1) and management review (clause 5.6). Required outputs of management review include decisions and actions that affect product improvements related to customer requirements. These improvements can help mitigate the risk of customer dissatisfaction.

To better understand the risk of customer dissatisfaction, quality managers need to be familiar with the organization's operations, the contributions of its units and divisions to development and production, the effect on key customers, and their requirements. Information systems should be integrated into the processes for producing products and services. This is important because both ISO 9001 and ISO 14001 require communication with customers and suppliers.

There are three international standards that deal with customer satisfaction: ISO 10001[3], which addresses customer satisfaction codes of conduct; ISO 10002[4], which addresses complaint handling; and ISO 10003[5], which provides a methodology for dispute resolution. These three standards can be used either independently or together. When used together they can be part of a broader, integrated framework for enhanced customer satisfaction.

3.2.7 Supply chain risk

Procurement managers must be concerned with managing outsourced products and services, sole supplier risks, delivery problems, quality of received products, inventory management, and design-and-documentation problems. A key to effective supply chain management is proactive communication with the suppliers.

Performance metrics used to measure the effectiveness of the supply chain consist of delivery performance, cycle time, inventory, cash management, and supply chain costs.

The following are factors used to develop each of these metrics. For measurement of delivery performance, gather data on on-time delivery, product quality, return rates, and experiences with supplier warranty management.

- *Cycle time,* which is measured by comparing promised vs. actual lead time, rework time, and length of the cycle
- *Inventory and cash management,* which is measured by inventory days of supply, day's sales outstanding, day's payables outstanding, and cash conversion time. The organization can share this data with key suppliers as a method of improving supply chain effectiveness.
- *Supply chain costs,* which consist of the cost of order management, inventory carrying costs, supply chain finance and planning, supply chain IT costs, and procurement department staffing

---

3. ISO 10001:2007, "Quality management—Customer satisfaction—Guidelines for codes of conduct for organizations," Geneva, Switzerland, 2007.
4. ISO 10002: 2004, "Quality management—Customer satisfaction—Guidelines for complaint handling in organizations," Geneva, Switzerland, 2004.
5. ISO 10003:2007, "Quality management—Customer satisfaction—Guidelines for dispute resolution external to organizations," Geneva, Switzerland, 2007.

TL 9000[6], the telecommunications management system, provides a model for important supplier data that telecommunications organizations should consider collecting. Common measurements are the number of problem reports, problem-report/fix-response time, overdue problem reports, report fix responsiveness measurements, and on-time delivery. Hardware measurements are the return rates of various products and system outage measurements. Software measurements consist of system outage measurements and installation and maintenance factors such as release application aborts, patch quality, and update quality. Service measurements consist of installation, maintenance and repair measurements, and customer support service. Some of these measurements may be of value to organizations outside of the telecommunications industry.

3.2.8 Revenue recognition risk

Revenue recognition risk is a financial term that can affect costs and profits. It consists of tracing products from sales through production to delivery and accounts receivable. Revenue recognition is affected by accounts payable problems, accounts receivable problems, revenues recorded before delivery, quotation-to-cash errors, spreadsheet errors, and outdated or incomplete pricing information.

The quality manager has a major role in controlling the effectiveness of the revenue recognition process. There is an overlap between quality and financial management systems that includes product realization, costs, sales, invoices, payments, inventory management, and delivery.

In a case study of organizations that link quality and financial management as part of their SOX compliance efforts, researchers found that processes familiar to QMS and EMS managers, such as shipping, receiving, nonconforming products, inventory control, and customer focus, were valuable inputs used in the revenue recognition process.[7] Another organization outlined in the case study spent a lot of time analyzing the shipping process. Data from shipping were a direct input into accounts receivables and revenue recognition. Another organization confirmed that outputs from the customer service and order processes are adequate and effective for the needs of the finance department.

---

6. TL 9000, "Quality Management System Measurements Handbook," Release 4.0, QuEST Forum, *www.questforum.org,* 2007.
7. Sandford Liebesman, "QMSs and EMSs Support Financial Management Systems," *Quality Progress*, March 2006, 83–85.

In many companies, revenue recognition problems have a major effect on the organization's earnings. Corrections may result in a restatement of earnings that may trigger a falling stock price. A major risk in the revenue recognition process is the use of spreadsheets, although the vast majority of organizations use them.[8]

There is also a risk of material misstatements due to fraud relating to revenue recognition. The auditor should test the controls specifically established to prevent and detect fraud related to a material misstatement in the company's revenue recognition processes.

3.2.9 Information security risk

Information security risks include viruses, unsecured files, inaccurate financial records and reporting, poor change control, information retrieval errors, overuse of spreadsheets in information management, use of contractors and consultants, the introduction of new technology (hardware, software, network, etc.), industrial espionage, and fraud.

ISO/IEC 27001:2005[9] was designed to provide management of information security. It requires the selection of adequate and proportionate security controls that protect information assets and give confidence to interested parties. The standard applies to all types of organizations (e.g., commercial enterprises, government agencies, nonprofit organizations). ISO/IEC 27001:2005 specifies the requirements for establishing, implementing, operating, monitoring, reviewing, maintaining, and improving a documented information security management system within the context of the organization's overall business risks. It specifies requirements for the implementation of security controls customized to the needs of individual organizations. It's intended for several different uses, including formulating security requirements and objectives, ensuring that security risks are cost-effectively managed, ensuring compliance with laws and regulations, and providing a process framework to assure that the specific security objectives of an organization are met.

The standard encourages definition of a new information security management process, its use by management to determine the status of information security management activities, and its use by the internal and external auditors to determine the degree of compliance with the policies, directives, and standards.

---

8. *www.revenuerecognition.com*
9. ISO/IEC 27001:2005, "Specification for an Information Security Management System." Geneva, Switzerland, 2005.

Finally, ISO/IEC 27001 defines methods of communicating information about security policies, directives, standards, and procedures to customers, trading partners, and other organizations with whom they interact for operational or commercial reasons. ISO/IEC 27001 is discussed in more detail in chapter 4.

3.2.10 Logistics risk

Homeland security affects the transport of shipping containers. A risk of major concern to organizations today is the risk caused by the threat to our country's security. The search for concealed weapons of mass destruction will slow shipping processes. In the future, all containers will be screened, identified, and traced from the country of origin to the purchasing organization.

The following are factors that affect logistics risk:

- Transportation of raw materials
- Transportation of completed products
- Damaged shipped products
- Delays causing the organization to miss customer on-time delivery requirements
- Delays causing under stocking of materials
- Homeland security information requirements

New tools have to be developed to perform the screening and tracing economically and without supply chain disruption. After the product is produced, you have the reverse problem: shipping to the customer. The problem goes beyond hard goods. Software is at risk due to viruses spread by people who wish to hurt the economy.

3.2.11 Risks from natural disasters

In the past few years we have experienced a number of natural disasters: major hurricanes, floods, fires, earthquakes, contamination, epidemics, etc. Business continuity requires safekeeping of enterprise information in protected storage. Organizations should plan for disaster recovery and business continuity (BC) to ensure that all documents are retained and available to investigating agencies, potential material events are considered and covered, and audit documents are safe for the seven-year period required by SOX.

Information technology (IT) plays an important role in the BC process. IT procedures should be specifically defined to ensure that the organization will operate in a timely and effective manner in the case of a disaster. Members of the IT organization should be part of the BC development team.

IT must provide safekeeping and protective storage of enterprise information. It must manage, secure, and provide safety against all disasters. The methodology is to regularly copy information into an off-premises backup system in a secure location. Data at this location should be tested for accuracy on a regular basis. ISO/IEC 27001 provides controls for BC management.

The following are components of a business continuity plan (BCP):

- Business risk and impact analysis
- Prepared activities documented for emergencies
- Initial response activities for a disaster event
- Procedures for managing business recovery processes
- Plans for training at multiple levels
- Procedures for keeping the BCP updated

In addition, the BCP should be exercised periodically to ensure that it operates correctly. Some questions an organization should ask about its BCP plan are:

- Does a written plan exist to ensure continuation of critical information processes in the event of computer failure?
- Is the plan updated and tested annually or when significant modifications to computer hardware, software, or application systems occur?
- Does the organization test the back-up media to ensure accurate restoration?
- Are copies of the plan and the back-up information retained off site?
- Are application programs, application data, and operating system software backed up periodically?

An example of an effective BCP plan is an audit of an organization that manufactures electronic equipment in three different locations. The audit revealed that the core of its plan is the development of tools to quickly transfer product manufacture from one location to the other two locations. The IT system is a key to the process that maintains the essential documentation of all manufacturing processes in each location. In addition, the manufacturing equipment is identical in all locations and could be quickly transformed to handle the other products.

3.3 RISK ANALYSIS METHODOLOGY

First, the organization must determine its risk appetite and risk tolerance so that all members of the organization can understand the risk philosophy. Once this is decided, there are tools to determine risk levels and manage the identified risks. One key tool for managing risk is an organization's set of controls. These are especially important for SOX compliance, which includes financial controls at the entity and activity levels.

3.3.1 Risk appetite

The starting point for determining an organization's risk appetite is for top management to understand the risks inherent in its existing business and its capabilities of managing them. The organization should also consider the effect of past events and the reactions of the key stakeholders to the events. This is called the organization's risk profile. An important related determination is the risk capacity of the organization. This is the maximum potential effect of a risk event that the organization can withstand.

Risk appetite is the amount of risk that an entity is willing to accept. In terms of SOX compliance, risk appetite reflects the "tone at the top." It is the measure of the risk-reward trade-off within the business and a major consideration in shaping the control environment of the organization's COSO response. Risk assessments beyond the boundaries of the risk appetite should result in preventive or corrective actions.

Risk appetite plays a key role in maximizing return on capital invested because it acts as a driver for allocation of capital to identified risks. Improving the understanding of risk appetite leads to a more efficient allocation of capital across the organization.[10] Risk appetite should be a function of the capacity to bear risk. Constraints on risk appetite include the capital needed to maintain support of the target agency's rating and regulatory capital requirements.

On the other hand, risk tolerance relates to the entity's specific objectives. It's the amount of variation relative to these objectives that an entity is willing to accept. Risk tolerance varies from department to department in an organization. While risk *appetite* is a broad, entity-wide concept, risk *tolerance* has a narrower focus. An organization may have different risk tolerances for its various operating units. However, when the individual risk tolerances are combined, they should fall within the overall risk appetite set by top management and the board.

Figure 3.1 depicts the relationship between risk profile, risk capacity, and risk tolerance, which are the major inputs to risk appetite.

---

10. "Why Is Risk Appetite Important?" Lloyd's, *www.lloyds.com*

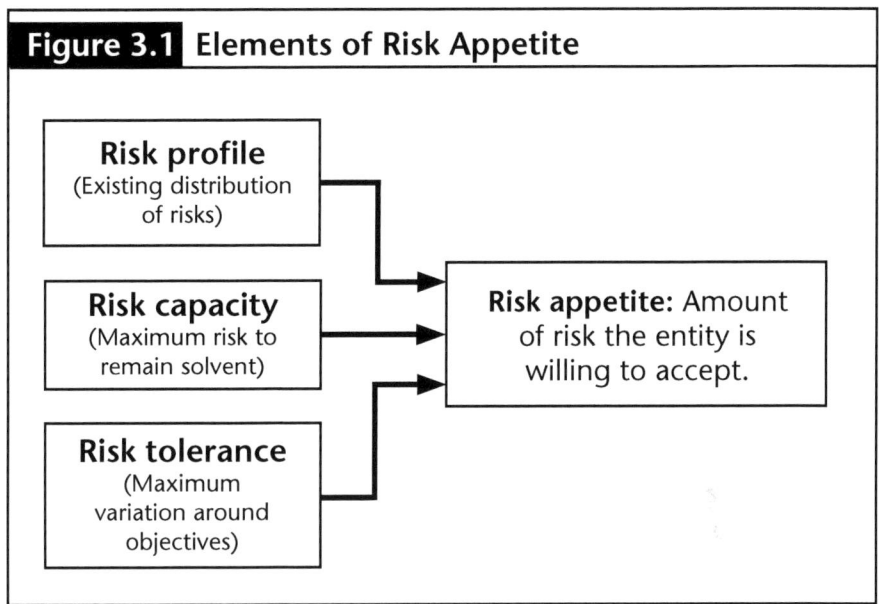

Figure 3.1 Elements of Risk Appetite

3.3.2 The use of controls

One key tool for managing risk is the organization's set of controls. Controls are especially important for compliance to SOX. Auditors test the controls as a key part of the compliance process. The financial controls are at two levels: entity and activity. Quality and environmental controls are also at these two levels and appear as "shall" statements in ISO 9001 and ISO 14001. "Shall" statements are often accompanied by requirements to submit a quality record. Some process performances requirements also include records of results that can be used to identify impending risks.

Examples of entity-level controls are human resources policies, codes of conduct, communication strategies, accounting policies, the management's risk assessment process, organizational structure, and contract review. Contract review requirements are related to quality requirements in ISO 9001:2008, clause 7.2.2.

Activity-level controls include reconciliation of general ledger to subsidiary ledgers, automated data validation and edit checks, limited access to confidential information, numbered transactions prior to entry, and review and approval of paper-based information prior to input. Quality controls at the activity level include control of nonconforming product (ISO 9001 clause 8.3), design-and-development validation (ISO 9001 clause 7.3.6), corrective and preventive action (ISO 9001 clauses 8.5.2 and 8.5.3), and identification of significant environmental aspects (ISO 14001 clause 4.3.1).

3.4 RISK MANAGEMENT PROCESS

Risk management consists of activities to identify and analyze risks that may prevent achievement of objectives. Effective risk assessment requires:

- Definition of the organization's objectives
- Assurance of the compatibility of the objectives
- Identification of risks to achieving objectives
- Judgment of which risks are critical. (Use a risk analysis matrix to determine criticality of the risk.)

- The use of risk management tools to mitigate risks. Examples of these tools include:
  - Objectives, risk, controls, and alignment (ORCA) process
  - ISO 9001 improvement process
  - Failure mode and effects analysis (FMEA)
  - Fault-tree analysis (FTA)
  - Risk control matrix
  - Risk analysis matrix

3.4.1 Risk analysis matrix

In a risk analysis matrix, the consequences and likelihood of each identified risk is estimated. These are then entered into the risk analysis matrix, as shown in figure 3.2.

After the level of concern is determined for each risk, preventive actions can be implemented for the extreme and high risks. ISO 9001 requires a procedure that:

- Determines potential risks and their causes
- Evaluates the need for action to prevent occurrence. (The risk analysis matrix is often used for this activity.)
- Determines and implements necessary actions
- Records results of corrective and preventive actions
- Reviews corrective and preventive actions taken

Figure 3.2 Risk Analysis Matrix

	Consequences				
Likelihood	**Insignificant**	**Minor**	**Moderate**	**Major**	**Catastrophic**
Almost certain	Moderate	High	High	Extreme	Extreme
Likely	Moderate	Moderate	High	High	Extreme
Possible	Low	Moderate	Moderate	High	Extreme
Unlikely	Low	Moderate	Moderate	Moderate	High
Rare	Low	Low	Moderate	Moderate	Moderate

Reference: *Designing an Effective Risk Matrix* by Henry Ozog and Judy Perry (ISOMOSAIC, 2002)

3.4.2 ORCA

Greg Hutchins[11] suggests using ORCA as an organizational risk assessment methodology. ORCA is a common organizational risk assessment methodology. It requires organizations to articulate organizational objectives (O), identify and broadly assess risks (R), build in balanced controls to manage organizational risk (C), and ensure alignment of objectives, risks, and controls across the entire enterprise (A).

After the risk assessment is conducted, senior management and operational managers can develop strategies to manage risks and execute business decisions. Risk management strategies include avoidance, mitigation, acceptance, diversification, and control.

3.4.3 ISO 9001 improvement process

Clause 8.5.1 of ISO 9001 includes an improvement loop that requires defining the quality policy, performing management system planning, defining measurable objectives, reviewing audit results, analysis of data, performing corrective and preventive actions, using management review to determine status of the management system, and instituting improvements.

The ISO 9001 risk management process focuses on analysis of data, corrective and preventive action, and management review. Trend data are used to identify opportunities for corrective and preventive actions, and management review results

---

11. Greg Hutchins, *Value-Added Auditing* (Quality Plus Engineering, 2003).

in changes to the management system and possible changes to quality and business objectives. The loop is repeated on a continuing basis resulting in ongoing system improvement.

3.4.4 Failure mode and effects analysis (FMEA)

FMEA is a method for risk prioritization and taking of preventive actions aimed at risk reduction. It's used to examine potential failures in products or processes and helps select remedial actions that reduce risks.

FMEA is a bottom-up procedure that starts by identifying each failure mode at the lowest level of the hierarchy. These are called local effects. The methodology is then used to evaluate failure modes in steps up the structure of the product or process until the highest level, the system level, is reached.

At each level, FMEA starts with a description of the parts of a system. Next, the consequences of each part failure are determined. A risk analysis matrix is used to evaluate the level of concern for each potential failure. Also determined is the ability of controls to detect failures. Actions are identified that could eliminate or reduce the occurrence of failures or improve their detectability. Finally, at each level, FMEA institutes changes to processes and products which are incorporated to avoid potential failures.

Carl S. Carlson, senior reliability engineer, ReliaSoft Corp.,[12] describes an eleven-step process for developing an effective FMEA process. He starts with the development of strategic and resource plans, then describes generic and program specific FMEAs. Next, he includes the design management reviews, quality audits, supplier FMEAs, methods of execution, and follow-up of recommended actions. His final steps are to include software support, linkage to other processes, and testing and follow-up of field failures.

Failure mode, effects, and criticality analysis (FMECA) is an extension of FMEA that includes a criticality analysis similar to the process described in the risk analysis matrix. The results are an identification of the failure modes with the highest likelihood of occurrence and the worst consequences.

3.4.5 Fault-tree analysis (FTA)

FTA is a top-down procedure that starts by identifying specific failure modes at the highest level of system or product structure. For each failure mode, a tree-

---

12.   Carl S. Carlson, "FMEA Success Factors: An Effective FMEA Process," *Reliability Edge*, Volume 6, Issue 1, ReliaSoft Publishing, Tucson, AZ, 2005.

like structure is developed that enables traceability to its root causes. Hence, the analyst can start with the system or product failure modes, identify the most consequential failure modes, and then identify problems at the lower levels that can be corrected to reduce the likelihood of system or product failure.

FTA uses logic diagrams to show graphically the structure of the system and the hazards that can occur at the highest level. At each lower level, specific problems are depicted with the single or multiple contributing factors. The graphic structure makes it easy to picture the causes and effects of the problems at each level. In some cases, multiple events must occur to cause the problem. These are depicted using "and" gates in the fault tree. In other cases only one of a number of events must occur to cause a failure. These are depicted as "or" gates.

FTA gives the risk analyst the ability to start at the highest level of the system, identify the worst consequences to the system and make corrections to problems at the lower levels that will greatly improve the functioning of the system. It's an approach that can be used by auditors to determine the best method for "top-down, risk-based" analysis of financial risks.

3.4.6 Risk control matrix[13]

The risk control matrix is a tool used to manage the risk of a specific process. Controls are set up to determine the status of the individual risks to the process. The risk control matrix gives management a picture of the most recent results of the control assessment. An example of a risk control matrix is shown in figure 3.3.

Closing the books is a methodology for combining the monthly income statement and financial statements to provide a consolidated monthly financial report for the company. In the example in figure 3.3, the risk is that the statement may contain material or immaterial misstatements or omissions. The control objective is no misstatements or omissions. The control used is a review of intercompany account balances, currency translation adjustments, and prior and current year accumulated deficit balances.

As the elements in figure 3.3 are hard to read, the following list contains the elements in the figure:
- Process (close the books)
- Key process number (1.1, 1.2)
- Risk (misstatements)

---

13. "How to Standardize Documentation for Internal Controls," Protiviti Inc., *www.protiviti.com.*

Figure 3.3 Risk Control Matrix

Key Process Number	Process	Risk Number	Risk	Control Objective	Control Number	Control Description	Control Owner	Process Narrative	Control Category	Control Type	Primary or Secondary	Control Frequency	Design Assessment
1.1	Close the books.	1	Financial statements may contain material or immaterial misstatements or omissions.	Financial statements do not contain material or immaterial misstatements or omissions.	1	Various review activities are performed throughout the process to verify financial data. These activities include the finance department's review of intercompany account balances for discrepancies, review of currency translation adjustments, and review of prior and current year accumulated deficit balances.	JH Doe	A2	Detective	Manual	Secondary	Monthly	Adequate
1.2					2	The accounting manager reviews all journal entries.	JH Doe	A3	Detective	Manual	Primary	Twice weekly	Inadequate

Process: Close the books. COSO objective: Integrity of financial reporting. Financial reporting element: All financial reporting elements.

- Control objective. (no misstatements)
- Control description. (Various review activities during close, accounting manager reviews all journal entries.)
- Control owner (John Doe)
- Process narrative (A.2, A.3)
- Control category (detective)
- Control type (manual)
- Primary or secondary control (secondary, primary)
- Frequency (monthly, twice weekly)
- Design assessment (adequate, inadequate)

3.5 RISK ELEMENTS IN PUBLISHED STANDARDS

There are a number of standards that address risk management and risk tools, including ISO 9001 and ISO 14001.[14] The focus in ISO 9001 is on measurable objectives and applying them throughout the management system. Data are gathered with respect to these objectives through a monitoring-and-measurement process. After data analysis, an improvement process is initiated and actions to reduce risk through the management review process. ISO 14001 focuses on significant aspects that may result in high risks. Figure 3.4 contains the ISO 9001 and ISO 14001 clauses that support risk management.

3.5.1 ISO 14971:2007: Risk management of medical devices[15]

Although ISO 14971 provides a methodology specifically for risk management of medical devices, it's also applicable in other environments. The standard covers risk management during the entire life cycle of products. This includes identifying hazardous situations and the evaluation of risk for these situations, controlling and reducing risks, and evaluating residual risks after implementation of control measures.

---

14. The following standards contain risk management guidance: ISO 31000: 2009 (risk management), ISO 9004, ISO 14001, ISO 14971 (medical devices), AS9100, ISO/PAS 28001 (supply chain), ISO 13824 (structures), ISO 17666 (space systems), ISO 16085 (software and systems), ISO 27005 (information security), IEC 60300-3-9 (dependability) and OHSA 18001 (health and safety management).
15. ISO 14971, "Medical devices—Application of risk management to medical devices," the International Organization for Standardization, Geneva, Switzerland, 2007.

Figure 3.4 ISO 9001 and ISO 14001 Support of Risk Management

Risk assessment	ISO 9001 and ISO 14001 clauses	
■ Establishment of objectives, linked at different levels and internally consistent.	4.1 (last paragraph)	Control of outsourced processes
	5.4.1	Quality objectives
■ Identification, analysis, and management of risks to achieving objectives.	5.6	Management review
	6.3	Infrastructure
■ Mechanisms to deal with change and the risks relevant to change.	7.2	Customer-related processes
	7.4	Purchasing
Effective risk assessment requires:	8.2	Monitoring and measurement
	8.4	Analysis of data
■ Definition of the objectives	8.5	Improvement
■ Determination of the compatibility of the objectives ■ Identification of risks to achieving the objectives ■ Determination of risks associated with change ■ Judgment as to which risks are critical ■ Determination of actions to mitigate risks starting with the critical ones	ISO 14001 clauses 4.3.1 and 4.5.2	Environmental aspects and identification of significant aspects (ISO 14001 clause 4.3.1) Evaluation of compliance (ISO 14001 clause 4.5.2)

A risk management process is defined to include a risk management plan, risk analysis process, risk evaluation, risk control and production, and post-production activities. A risk management file is required to record essential activities throughout the life of a product.

The risk control process consists of determining and analyzing risk control options, selecting and implementing control measures, evaluating residual risks after control measures have been applied, and identifying and evaluating the remaining risks. The risk control process must include the product process and post-production activities. Prior to release of the product, a review of the risk management process must be completed and a report published.

ISO 14971 contains ten excellent annexes that provide details of the major topics covered in the standard. Annex D stands out because of its coverage of hazards and hazardous situations, risk estimation, risk acceptability, risk control, risk-benefit analysis, and overall risk evaluation.

3.6 A RISK MANAGEMENT CASE STUDY

Case study 3.1 in appendix B was provided by Linda Ellrodt of the Juran Institute. It consists of a risk management project at a major research and teaching hospital. The risk considered was the risk and consequences of patients falling. Changes were made to the patient interventions and assessment tool. The changes resulted in a 10 percent reduction in several categories of patient falls. This case study provided an example of an organization satisfying two major types of risks: compliance risk and operational risk.

3.7 SUMMARY OF CHAPTER 3

Risk management must start by defining the organization's objectives. These should be measurable as required by ISO 9001. Risks are obstacles that impede progress toward achieving these objectives. Organizations need to determine their risk appetite and risk tolerance to maintain a consistent risk philosophy. The organization then determines risk levels by combining the likelihood of an event and its consequences in a risk analysis matrix. In a SOX-compliant process, controls should be selected using a top-down, risk-based approach and tested to identify deficiencies and possible material misstatements.

3.8 CHAPTER 3 EXERCISES: RISK IDENTIFICATION

The tables below contain the factors affecting each of the seven major risk categories. For your organization determine the likelihood, the consequences, and the risk level for each item.

Table 3.1	Risk of Ineffective Management Systems		
Risk	Likelihood (Rare, unlikely, possible, likely, or almost certain)	Consequences (Insignificant, minor, moderate, major, or catastrophic)	Risk level (Low, moderate, high, or extreme)
Poor management practices			
Poor human resources practices			
Lack of effective management tools			
Data-processing errors			
Ineffective call centers			
Poor marketing strategies			
Poor contract administration			
Customer communication issues			
Design-and-development problems			
Other (specify)			

Table 3.2	Customer Satisfaction Risk		
Risk	Likelihood (Rare, unlikely, possible, likely, or almost certain)	Consequences (Insignificant, minor, moderate, major, or catastrophic)	Risk level (Low, moderate, high, or extreme)
Poor communication			
Delivery problems			
Product quality			
Design problems			
Repair problems			
Customer satisfaction			
Other (specify)			

Table 3.3	Supply Chain Risks		
Risk	Likelihood (Rare, unlikely, possible, likely, or almost certain)	Consequences (Insignificant, minor, moderate, major, or catastrophic)	Risk level (Low, moderate, high, or extreme)
Product quality			
Poor communication			
Outsourcing large number of processes			
Ineffective supplier management			
Sole supplier			
Design/documentation errors			
Overstock or understock			
Other (specify)			

Table 3.4	Revenue Recognition Risk		
Risk	Likelihood (Rare, unlikely, possible, likely, or almost certain)	Consequences (Insignificant, minor, moderate, major, or catastrophic)	Risk level (Low, moderate, high, or extreme)
Accounts payable			
Accounts receivable			
Revenue recorded before delivery			
Order-to-cash problems			
Spreadsheet errors			
Outdated or incomplete pricing information			
Other (specify)			

Table 3.5	Information Security Risk		
Risk	Likelihood (Rare, unlikely, possible, likely, or almost certain)	Consequences (Insignificant, minor, moderate, major, or catastrophic)	Risk level (Low, moderate, high, or extreme)
Viruses			
Unsecured files			
Inaccurate financial records and reporting			
Poor change control			
Information retrieval errors			
Overuse of spreadsheets			
Use of contractors and consultants			
Introduction of new technology			
Industrial espionage			
Fraud			
Other (specify)			

Table 3.6 Logistics Risks			
Risk	Likelihood (Rare, unlikely, possible, likely, or almost certain)	Consequences (Insignificant, minor, moderate, major, or catastrophic)	Risk level (Low, moderate, high, or extreme)
Transportation of raw materials			
Transportation of completed products			
Damaged shipped products			
Delays causing the organization to miss on-time delivery			
Delays causing under stocking of materials			
Homeland security information requirements			
Other (specify)			

Table 3.7 Risks from Natural Disasters			
Risk	Likelihood (Rare, unlikely, possible, likely, or almost certain)	Consequences (Insignificant, minor, moderate, major, or catastrophic)	Risk level (Low, moderate, high, or extreme)
Hurricanes			
Floods			
Fires			
Earthquakes			
Infrastructure problems			
Contamination			
Epidemics			
Other (specify)			

Chapter 4

The Importance of Information Technology in Effective Business Operations

4.1 INTRODUCTION

An effective information technology (IT) process is critical to the operation of any business. Multiple software applications are needed to run a business. These include financial, sales, customer service and support, inventory management, enterprise resource planning (ERP), and marketing. IT is also important to Sarbanes-Oxley (SOX) compliance. This is because the correct and safe storage of data is critical to maintaining and analyzing data and protecting important corporate records. SOX also makes fragmented business management systems even more costly and problematic.

4.2 IT SYSTEM STRUCTURE

It's important to understand the structure and complexity of a typical IT management system. A computer has five major parts: the control system, memory storage devices, input and output devices, software, and networking systems. Note that the parts described may not be included in all IT systems. Organizations must fit their IT systems to the needs of their management systems.

The control system consists of the central processing unit (CPU) and the arithmetic logic unit (ALU). The CPU retrieves instructions and data, decodes the instructions, and carries them out in the ALU. Multiple CPUs can be used to reduce processing time.

Memory storage devices consist of physical storage devices and random access memory (RAM). The primary physical storage devices are hard disk drives. Other memory devices include floppy disk drives, DVDs, CD-ROMs, and USB drives.

Input/output devices are used to transfer data in and out of the system. They include work stations, terminals, servers, and communication devices. Work stations are desktop machines that enhance mathematical and graphical abilities. A terminal is online equipment that is common input device. Terminals include keyboards and monitors that allow users display of inputs and computer outputs. Servers support the network by permitting users to share data, peripherals, and programs. Communication devices allow transfer of information among computers. Examples are multiplexers, modems, routers, and bridges.

IT software consists of the operating system, applications software, and security software. The operating system acts as the interface between applications software and the hardware. It manages the access to computer resources. The main forms of computer software are operating systems, libraries, data, user interfaces, and applications.

The operating system (OS) software manages sharing resources and provides access to the resources. The OS processes data and inputs and manages tasks and internal system resources. The OS controls and allocates memory, prioritizes system requests, controls input and output devices, facilitates networking, and manages file systems. The operating system is a platform for other software and applications.

Applications software provides the capability to perform tasks central to the functioning of the IT system. Some examples of software applications are word processing, spreadsheets, databases, e-mail servers, media players, and user-written software. Specific applications include financial management, customer relationship management, and supply chain management.

Security software protects software from unauthorized activities. It must be designed and implemented to protect data and other resources. Security software plays an important role in system backup and recovery from system failure. In addition, there are virus and worm protection, internet security, user account management, and firewall protection.

Computer networking is concerned with communication between computer systems or devices. Specifically this is concerned with routers, routing protocols, and networking over the Internet. A computer network is a set of computers or devices connected to each other with the ability to exchange data. Specific examples are local area networks, wide area networks, wireless networks, intranets, and extranets.

4.3 DATA STORAGE, MANAGEMENT, AND ANALYSIS

A data warehouse consolidates data that are spread across the organization. This is an important tool for any organization. In the current competitive environment, organizations must gather, analyze, and store large amounts of data on products, services, personnel, customers, competitors, government requirements, research and development, and other topics. The data must be stored in a manner that makes them readily accessible to key personnel of the organization.

A centralized data repository is also a requirement for SOX compliance. The data warehousing system must address data quality and data cleansing and should result in easier compliance. This may provide a competitive advantage to the organization.

IT solutions for document and records management help with ISO 9001:2008 records management and SOX compliance. Some examples of key documents and records are CEO/CFO sign-offs in SOX sections 302 and 404 and archived e-mails and attached documents in chronological sequence in SOX section 404. These may be used to prove that internal controls are appropriate. IT can provide SOX section 802 with an audit trail that prevents altering, concealing, or destroying documents.

An effective data storage system should include data mining. One result of this activity is the development of new insights into company competitive operation. Data mining can reveal patterns and correlations between apparently unrelated sets of data. These patterns provide new hypotheses for the cause-and-effect relationships throughout the enterprises' value chain. This is very important for compliance with clause 8.4 of ISO 9001, which relates to data analysis. This clause also requires the recognition of trends in data.

A data storage system can also be used to help identify and improve areas for control as required in SOX section 404. Data mining is a tool for internal auditing of the controls and identification of data tampering. For SOX section 409, data mining can also detect unforeseen patterns.

4.4 TRANSACTION SYSTEMS

Transaction systems are used to collect and store the transactions of an organization. Each transaction can be modified and retrieved at any time. Five common transaction systems are supply chain management (SCM), ERP, business continuity planning (BCP), customer relationship management (CRM), and the order-to-cash cycle. As examples of the role IT plays in transaction management, we will discuss SCM, BCP, and CRM.

Supply chain management is the process of planning, implementing, and controlling the operations of a supply chain. It includes all movement and storage of raw materials, work-in-progress inventory, and the shipment of finished goods to points-of-consumption. It includes the supply process, supply chain inventory, and supply analytics. ISO 10014[1] provides tables with a series of questions that can help an organization develop an effective SCM process.

SCM has several risks. A vendor's potential inability to supply materials on a timely basis is one of them. On-time delivery is a key measure used by organizations to determine the level of service provided by a supplier. It's also used as a metric for organizations that comply with TL 9000.[2]

A second risk is the potential inability of a vendor to supply products that consistently meet its customers' production specifications. There are two problems that can arise: either the specifications are flawed or the suppler can't satisfy them. A cooperative effort is the best way of managing these risks. As stated in the quality management principle, "mutually beneficial supplier relationships: the organization and its suppliers are independent and a mutually beneficial relationship enhances the ability of both to create value."[3]

Enterprise resource planning is the process of monitoring and evaluating raw materials and related supplier quality and performance by eliminating waste, reducing quality problems, and streamlining the manufacturing process. It's an enterprise wide system that captures data at the point of generation for core business processes. Typical processes included in an ERP system are finance, manufacturing, SCM, human resources, customer relations, data warehousing, and inventory management.

In a manufacturing environment, ERP includes the processes for engineering, bills of material, scheduling, capacity, workflow management, quality control, cost management, and manufacturing flow. The data flowing into and out of these processes are essential to effective manufacturing operations.

---

1. ISO 10014:2006, "Quality management systems—A guideline for realizing financial and economic benefits." International Organization for Standardization. Geneva, Switzerland, 2006.
2. *TL 9000 Quality Management System Measurements Handbook Release 4.0* (QuEST Forum, 2006).
3. ISO 9000:2005, "Quality management systems—Fundamentals and vocabulary." International Organization for Standardization. Geneva, Switzerland, 2005.

Good data management is required for an effective inventory system. The data required include raw materials, work-in-progress, finished goods, and repaired product. In a telecommunications circuit pack manufacturing process, raw materials include resistors, capacitors, components, solder paste, solder bath, and raw circuit boards. The raw materials are placed on the circuit boards, tested, inspected, and placed in finished-goods inventory. Finished product is shipped to the customers out of this inventory. Product returned from the customer is repaired using diagnostic testing, replacement of components as needed, end-product testing, and quality control. Repaired units may be returned to the customer or placed in special inventory. Product is shipped out of inventory using control processes such as first-in/first-out, last-in/first-out, or special selection processes.

Business continuity planning is a process used to create a plan for recovery and restoration of functions after an extended disruption. It can also help an organization prepare for accidents or incidents that could jeopardize its operations and even its existence.

A typical BCP process starts with a business risk and impact analysis. The organization must identify the risks to its corporate objectives and determine priorities for each risk. Next, the affected corporate activities for each risk are identified and documented. Then the initial response procedures and the method of managing the business recovery processes are described. The BCP must include training of responding individuals at all affected levels. Finally, the process must include procedures for keeping the BCP updated.

As an example of a BCP process, assume that a tornado touched down and destroyed one of three factories belonging to Company X. Assume that the products manufactured at this location are different from the ones built at the other two locations. The first order of business is to assure the safety of all employees. Local, state, and national authorities need to be notified. Then the business recovery process is initiated. As part of the BCP preparation, important corporate data had previously been copied daily and sent to a safe area off-site. Company X had created a process by which each location could be used to manufacture the products at the other locations. This process is initiated using the relevant data that had been saved off line. Personnel had been trained in the recovery procedures.

Note that SOX requires safekeeping of enterprise information and internal audit-relevant documentation. In addition, internal control documents must be safely stored. This should be done as part of the off-premises storage of data.

4.5 KEY SOX SECTIONS AND IT

There are nine sections of the SOX that address definitions of IT's role in compliant organizations. Each one is described below with an indication of how IT is important in compliance to SOX.[4]

- *Section 103: Auditing, Quality Control, Standards, and Rules.* Requires public accounting firms to prepare and maintain audit work papers and other information related to audit reports for at least seven years. These must be in sufficient detail to support audit results. This includes the scope of the auditor's testing of the internal control structure and procedures of the issuer. IT processes are key to proper storage of this information.

- *Section 201: Auditor Independence.* Prevents firms that audit a company's books from also providing it with IT services. This includes bookkeeping accounting records or financial statements of the audit, financial information systems design, and implementation or appraisal or valuation services.

- *Section 301: Public Company Audit Committees.* Requires provision of systems or procedures that let whistleblowers communicate confidentially with the audit committee. The system must include anonymous methods of receipt, retention, and treatment of complaints regarding accounting, internal accounting controls, or auditing activities.

- *Section 302: Corporate Responsibility for Financial Reports* and *Section 404: Management Assessment of Internal Control.* Allows IT to provide the required secure records of effective control. Section 404 requires control over changes to systems that have an effect on the financial reporting of an organization. Proof of SOX compliance requires saving all the documents and work papers used to create financial reports and other publications produced for the general public. Thus, IT plays an important role in establishing and maintaining an adequate internal control structure and procedures for financial reporting and providing support for the assessment of the internal control structure and procedures for financial reporting.

- *Section 409: Real-Time Disclosures.* Requires companies to disclose information on material changes in the financial condition or operations of the issuer on a rapid and current basis. IT maintains this information and must have methods to provide this information quickly.

---

4. HR 3763, Sarbanes-Oxley Act of 2002, 107th Congress, July 24, 2002.

- *Section 802: Criminal Penalties for Altering Documents.* Requires protection against destruction, alteration, or falsification of records in federal investigations and bankruptcy. Accountants who conduct internal audits must maintain all audit or review work papers for a period of five years from the end of the fiscal period in which the audit or review was concluded.
- *Section 806: Protection for Employees of Publicly Traded companies.* A publicly traded company may not discharge, demote, suspend, threaten, harass, or in any other manner discriminate against a whistleblower.
- *Section 1102: Tampering with a Record or Otherwise Impeding an Official Inquiry.* Requires IT personnel to provide a secure means of protecting data. IT must have procedures for change control and information security. Note that sections 802 and 1102 are major concerns of the IT organization.

4.6 INFORMATION TECHNOLOGY'S ROLE IN SATISFYING INTERNAL CONTROL

Section 404 of SOX requires establishment and maintenance of an effective system of internal control. IT plays an important role in meeting these requirements.

IT provides uniform processing of transactions. Computer programs can automatically initiate the execution of transactions, and the consistency of computer processing can eliminate many clerical errors. However, automated processing may be subject to programming errors that can result in multiple incorrect processing of transactions.

Software can be developed to provide transaction trails that are useful for effective auditing of internal control. These trails may exist only for a short time and may be batched with other information.

There is a strong potential for increased management supervision of internal control. Computers provide the capability for analytical tools to review and supervise operations. One example is an increased ability to compare actual and budgeted operating ratios and reconciliations. Also, statistics can be gathered to monitor processing of data.

One major concern is the increased potential for errors and fraud. Special controls can be used to prevent unauthorized access to data or unauthorized use of key programs. Application programs can be changed, resulting in fraud. Segregation of functions may be more difficult because functions previously performed by individuals may now be performed by a single computer program under the control of one person.

Note that controls can be made more efficient using computer systems. The speed with which computer reports and other outputs can be produced can greatly enhance manual controls. Effectiveness depends on the timeliness and accuracy of the programs.

4.7 GENERAL IT CONTROLS

The IT control environment is generally maintained by a computer processing department. This is a service organization that should report to senior-level management and be independent of users. The department should also have no asset-custody function or transaction authority.[5]

Documentation supports and explains data processing applications and system development and is a key component of internal control. Documents should be secured in a library with controlled access. There should be uniform standards for narratives, flowcharting, coding, and modification. Operating and user documentation should describe setup, files and devices, inputs, messages, run times, recovery procedures, outputs, and controls.

System and program acquisition and development should be managed by a broad-based team of financial and operations managers, auditors, and IT professionals. The team should include participation by top management. It's also important to have all key organizations represented.

The authority and responsibility for computer processing must maintain the segregation of duties.[6] This can be difficult in computer systems because of the ability of computers to do multiple tasks. The organization should have standards for system design and programming, strict control of system changes, testing of new or modified programs, and procedures to detect unauthorized program changes.

Operational controls are needed to assure that IT is supporting an effective system of internal control. The controls should include disaster recovery and protection against loss of data, procedures for acquiring and implementing systems, controls over access to equipment and data files, and controls that ensure segregation of duties and responsibilities.

---

5. Asset Custody Function: If you own financial assets and do not have expertise or time to manage them, you usually seek a professional management service. For the asset custody function, the management service has physical control of the assets. These custodians have legal authority to hold your assets and are also responsible for reporting tax and legal implications to the appropriate government agencies.

6. An example of "segregation of duties" is the requirement that the person creating a financial payment is not the person who signs the check.

Application controls assure that specific tasks are done correctly. There should be controls over inputs, data acquisition, processing, recording, and outputs. It's important to have controls over reports generated as outputs of each application. There should be controls to assure that only authorized actions are included in each task. Some examples of applications are accounts receivable, accounts payable, invoices, and disbursements.

4.8 CONTROL ACTIVITIES[7]

Hardware controls are built into the equipment to detect and control errors. There should be storage protection to prevent unauthorized reading or writing in the CPU and associated programs. Other activities to consider include:

■ Diagnostic routine check for hardware problems
■ Input data read twice and compared
■ Duplicate circuits in Arithmetic-Logic Unit (ALU)
■ Peripheral devices return (echo) signals sent by CPU
■ File protection to prevent overwriting data storage media
■ Parity checks to verify data transfer
■ Regular preventive maintenance

Access controls prevent improper use or manipulation of data files and programs. Security controls can be used to protect against unauthorized access to data processing. Examples are passwords, identification numbers, and personal codes for online access. Physical entry into secure locations may be controlled using magnetic or optically scanned cards or biometric technologies. Other tools available for access control include:

■ Device access controls
■ System access log
■ Encryption of data before transmission
■ Callback from the computer before transmission of data
■ Controlled disposal of outdated documents
■ Automatic log-off of inactive terminals
■ Utility software restrictions that allow only security people to use the software

---

7. See Irvin N. Gleim and Wlliam A. Hillison, *Gleim's CPA Review, Auditing.* (Gleim Publications Inc., June 2001).

Input controls are important because they protect against the most error-prone activities. Some examples of input controls are edit checks, echo checks, completeness checks to verify that all data have been sent, and closed-loop verification by an operator. Echo checks are accomplished by sending back data over transmission or communication lines for comparison. This is used to verify that hardware is operating properly.

Processing controls are used to test the logic of processing data. Note that some input controls are also processing controls. For example, sign tests check that data in a field have the appropriate arithmetic sign. Audit trails should be created through the use of input-output logs, error listings, and transaction logs. Other controls include:

- Comparison of a record before and after updating
- Cross-footing compares an amount to the sum of its parts
- Zero-balance assures that the positive and negative amounts posted add to zero
- Internal header and trailer labels check that the correct files are processed
- Run-to-run control totals check critical amounts at designated points in a process
- End-of-file procedures to prevent premature closing of transaction files
- Concurrency controls prevent two or more programs from using a file simultaneously

Output controls are usually the responsibility of a data control group. Error listings and exception reports are reviewed by the group and sent to users for correction and resubmission. A log may be used for unusual interruptions, interventions, or other activities.

Risk management controls are used to protect against major risks to the system. These include backup and recovery, virus and worm protection, and Internet security. Backup and recovery policies and procedures start with reconstruction and recovery plans to regenerate important programs and databases. The organization should create backup files and store them off premises. These files can be used to reconstruct the system programs and data. The backup system should be periodically checked to ensure that it's operating correctly. It should also be fully protected against power failure. Finally, the planning should include the ability to process data at other sites.

Virus and worm protection are musts in today's environment. Preventive controls should ensure the use of clean and certified copies of software. Detective controls are used to identify virus and worm infestation. There are numerous suppliers of software for identification and elimination of viruses and worms. The organization needs to have corrective controls that ensure a clean backup is maintained and have a recovery plan in the case of infestation.

Internet security can be accomplished using an organizationwide network security policy. A key component of such a policy is that only authorized users have access to it. A methodology that assures secrecy of critical information should be used to prevent unauthorized or accidental modification of information. As part of the security process, user account management should assure that new accounts are added correctly, unused accounts are removed promptly, and passwords are changed periodically. Finally, an effective firewall should be used to separate the internal network from external networks and produce reports on Internet use, exception reports, and reports of system penetration.

4.9 INFORMATION SECURITY

Information security requires protecting information systems and the information contained in them. The risks to the information include unauthorized access, disclosure to unauthorized persons, destruction, unauthorized modification, and contamination. A major concern is protection against proprietary information falling into the hands of competitors.

ISO/IEC 27001[8] is a widely accepted standard that includes guidelines and controls for information security. The controls are based on legislative requirements and best practices for information security. The standard describes the design, implementation, and management of information security processes and controls throughout an organization. Essential controls include data protection and privacy of personal information, safeguarding of organizational records, and intellectual property rights. It also includes many requirements found in ISO 9001 and ISO 14001, such as document control, management review, and internal audit.

The plan-do-check-act (PDCA) cycle is the basic structure of the standard. The plan phase starts with an information security risk assessment, which must be based on the scope of the information management system. Everything of value to the organization must be determined and documented. This includes information processing and storage equipment, software, communications equipment, build-

---

8. ISO/IEC 27001:2005, "Information technology—Security techniques—Specification for an information security management system." International Organization for Standardization, Geneva, Switzerland, 2005.

ings, and other assets of the information system. A valuable tool for this effort is an assets register with a risk assessment of each item. The ISO 27001 risk assessment process is similar to the one described in chapter 3.

Risk appetite comes into play next. If the level of risk for an asset is greater than the organization's risk appetite, the organization must reduce the risk. Annex A of ISO/IEC 27000 contains a list of appropriate controls. ISO/IEC 27001 lists 130 controls in eleven categories, which are shown in figure 4.1.

Figure 4.1 Control Categories	
Number	**Control category**
1	Security policy: Direction and support of information security
2	Organization of assets and resources
3	Asset clarification and control
4	Personnel security
5	Physical and environmental security
6	Communications and operations management
7	Access control
8	Systems development and maintenance
9	Information security incident management
10	Business continuity management
11	Compliance to civil and criminal laws

Categories one and two focus on an organization's structure and personnel. A corporate-level security policy and security objectives are required. Review boards must be defined, and they must be available to all parties affected by the policy. The structure must include the responsibilities of each. Human resources personnel should help determine tasks and personnel requirements.

Categories three and seven address asset clarification and control. The requirement to maintain an asset register is covered here. The register must include the level of protection of each asset and who has access. Passwords, IT accounts, and user time outs are typical access controls.

Categories four and five cover physical and IT security. Equipment must be protected from unauthorized access online and in person. Encryption is one method of preventing unwanted intrusion.

Categories six and eight address networks and IT. Category six focuses on development planning and testing. These categories cover network design and vulnerability and back-up design.

Categories nine and ten describe actions that occur when things go wrong. Specifically, what must be done when security is breached? If the security failure is severe enough, the BCP may be initiated.

Category eleven deals with legal compliance. Is only approved equipment connected? Are all proper licenses available? Internal audits should be used to assure compliance.

ISO/IEC 27002[9] contains a set of information security controls describing best practices in information security. It addresses the following:

- Risk assessment and treatment
- Security policies
- Organization
- Asset management
- Human resources
- Communication and operations management
- Physical and environmental
- Access control
- Information systems acquisition, development, and maintenance
- Information security incident management
- Business continuity management
- Compliance

The United Kingdom Accreditation Service (UKAS) has developed a certification scheme to demonstrate compliance to ISO 27001. ISO/IEC 27002 provides the tools to help organizations obtain ISO 27001 certification, while ISO/IEC 27006[10] offers guidelines for the accreditation of organizations.

The following members of the ISO/IEC 27000 family are currently under development:

- ISO/IEC 27000 (standard vocabulary for family of standards)

9.   ISO/IEC 27002:2005, "Information technology—Security techniques—Code of practice for information security management," International Organization for Standardization, Geneva, Switzerland, 2005.
10.   ISO/IEC 27006:2007, "Information technology—Security techniques—Requirements for bodies providing audit and certification of information security management systems," International Organization for Standardization, Geneva, Switzerland, 2007.

- ISO/IEC 27003 (information security management system implementation guide)
- ISO/IEC 27004 (new standard for information security management)
- ISO/IEC 27005 (proposed standard for risk management)
- ISO/IEC 27007 (guide for auditing information security management systems)
- ISO/IEC 27011 (guideline for telecommunications in information security management systems)
- ISO/IEC 27799 (guidance on implementing ISO/IEC 27002 in the health care industry)

4.10 COBIT MANAGEMENT OF IT CONTROLS

The best tool for managing IT controls is Control Objectives for Information and Related Technology (CobIT), which was developed by the Information Systems Audit and Control Association[11] (ISACA) and published in 1996. The current issue is CobIT 4.1. Its primary purposes are to provide clear policies and practices for managing risk associated with IT and provide IT control information to the chief information officer (CIO).

The CobIT executive overview gives the following description of CobIT and its purposes: "CobIT is a framework and supporting tool set that allows managers to bridge the gap with respect to control requirements, technical issues and business risks, and communicate that level of control to stakeholders. CobIT enables the development of clear policies and good practice for IT control throughout organizations. CobIT is continuously kept up to date and harmonized with other standards and guidance. Hence, CobIT has become the integrator for IT good practices and the umbrella framework for IT governance that helps in understanding and managing the risks and benefits associated with IT. The process structure of CobIT and its high-level, business-oriented approach provide an end-to-end view of IT and the decisions to be made about IT."[12]

4.10.1 The CobIT framework[13]

The CobIT control framework is a management control system. It provides a link to business requirements, organizes IT into a process model, identifies IT resources, and defines management control objectives.

---

11. *www.isaca.org*
12. CobIT 4.1, Executive Overview, IT Governance Institute. *www.itgi.org.*
13. The latest version of the CobIT Framework is defined in CobIT 4.1, *Control Objectives for Information and Related Technology* (IT Governance Institute, 2007), *www.itgi.org.*

Figure 4.2 CobIT Framework

Domains
Plan and organize. (Strategy and tactics)
Acquire and implement. (Identify IT solutions)
Delivery and support. (Delivery of services)
Modify and evaluate. (Regular assessment)

The framework contains thirty-four IT processes in four domains. Figure 4.2 shows an overview of the CobIT framework.

The plan and organize domain covers strategy and tactics and is concerned with the ways IT can best contribute to the achievement of the business objectives. There are ten plan and organize process categories, as shown in figure 4.3.

Figure 4.3 Plan-and-Organize Process Categories

Number	Category
1	Define a strategic IT plan.
2	Define the information architecture.
3	Determine technological direction.
4	Define the IT processes, organization, and relationships.
5	Manage the IT investment.
6	Communicate management aims and direction.
7	Manage IT human resources.
8	Manage quality.
9	Assess and manage IT risks.
10	Manage projects.

The realization of an organization's strategic vision needs to be planned, communicated, and managed for different perspectives. This requires proper organization and the right technological infrastructure. This domain typically addresses the following management questions:

■ Are IT and the business strategies aligned?
■ Is the enterprise achieving optimum use of its resources?
■ Does everyone in the organization understand the IT objectives?

■ Are IT risks understood and being managed?
■ Is the quality of IT systems appropriate for business needs?

The second domain is acquire and implement. IT solutions need to be identified, developed or acquired, and implemented and integrated into the business management system. Changes in the existing systems are covered by this domain to make sure the solutions continue to meet the business objectives. There are seven acquire-and-implement categories, as shown in figure 4.4.

Figure 4.4	Acquire-and-Implement Categories

Number	Category
1	Identify automated solutions.
2	Acquire and maintain application software.
3	Acquire and maintain technology infrastructure.
4	Enable operation and use.
5	Procure IT resources.
6	Manage changes.
7	Install and accredit solutions and changes.

To realize the IT strategy, solutions need to be identified, developed, acquired, and implemented and integrated into the business process. In addition, changes in and maintenance of existing systems are covered by this domain to ensure that the solutions continue to meet business objectives. This domain typically addresses the following management questions:

■ Are new projects likely to deliver solutions that meet business needs?
■ Are new projects likely to be delivered on time and within budget?
■ Will the new systems work properly when implemented?
■ Will changes be made without upsetting current business operations?

The third domain is delivery and support. This domain is concerned with the delivery of required services, and includes service delivery, management of security and continuity, service support for users, and management of data and operational facilities. There are thirteen delivery and support process categories, as shown in figure 4.5.

Figure 4.5	Delivery-and-Support Process Categories
Number	**Category**
1	Define and manage service levels.
2	Manage third-party services.
3	Manage performance and capacity.
4	Ensure continuous service.
5	Ensure systems security.
6	Identify and allocate costs.
7	Educate and train users.
8	Manage service desk and incidents.
9	Manage the configuration.
10	Manage problems.
11	Manage data.
12	Manage the physical environment.
13	Manage operations.

The delivery and support domain typically addresses the following management questions:

■ Are IT services being delivered in line with business priorities?
■ Is the IT cost optimized?
■ Is the work force able to use the IT systems productively and safely?
■ Is there adequate confidentiality, integrity, and availability for information security?

The final domain is monitor and evaluate. All IT processes need to be regularly assessed for their quality and compliance with control requirements. This domain addresses performance management, monitoring of internal control, regulatory compliance, and governance. There are four monitor and evaluate categories, as shown in figure 4.6.

Figure 4.6	Monitor-and-Evaluate Categories
Number	**Category**
1	Monitor and evaluate IT performance.
2	Monitor and evaluate internal control.
3	Ensure compliance with external requirements.
4	Provide IT governance.

The monitor-and-evaluate domain typically addresses the following management questions:

- Is the IT performance measured to detect problems before it is too late?
- Does management ensure that internal controls are effective and efficient?
- Can IT performance be linked back to business goals?
- Are there adequate confidentiality, integrity, and availability controls in place?

4.10.2 CobIT information criteria

CobIT defines seven criteria that information gathered in the IT system must satisfy. Figure 4.7 lists the criteria and defines the key characteristics of each.

Figure 4.7 **CobIT Information Criteria**	
Criteria	**Characteristics**
Effectiveness	Information must be relevant and pertinent to business processes. It must be delivered in a timely, correct, consistent, and usable manner.
Efficiency	Information is provided through the most productive and economical use of resources.
Confidentiality	Sensitive data are protected from unauthorized disclosure.
Integrity	The data are accurate and complete and have maintained validity in accordance with business values and expectations.
Availability	Information is available when required. It is also concerned with the safeguarding of necessary resources and associated capabilities.
Compliance	The organization complies with laws, regulations, and contract arrangements. This includes externally imposed business criteria as well as internal policies.
Reliability	Appropriate information is provided to management to operate the entity and exercise its fiduciary and governance responsibilities.

Information criteria provide a bridge between what operational managers must execute and what executives need to govern effectively. Every enterprise uses IT to enable business initiatives and these can be represented as business goals. CobIT's appendix 1[14] provides a matrix of generic business goals and IT goals and shows how they map to the information criteria.

Management should optimize the use of available IT resources, including applications, information, infrastructure, and people. To discharge these responsibilities and achieve its objectives, management should understand the status of its enterprise architecture for IT and decide what governance and control it should provide.

4.11 CONTROLS FOR ELECTRONIC RECORDS AND SIGNATURES[15]

The Food and Drug Administration (FDA) produced Title 21 CFR Part 11 to help organizations prepare and control electronic records. Although the guidance is aimed at FDA-regulated organizations, it can be used by any organization that has chosen to maintain records or submit information electronically.

Part 11 describes criteria covering the trustworthiness and reliability of electronic records and signatures. The goal of compliance is to make them equivalent to paper records and handwritten signatures.

The first element of electronic records management is the validation of the computerized systems. Part 11 states that the organization should consider the effect the systems might have on the accuracy, reliability, integrity, availability, and authenticity of required records and signatures. Validation should also review the consistency of intended performance and the ability to identify invalid or altered records. The process should examine the organization's ability to generate accurate and complete copies of records in physical and electronic format. Finally, system access must be limited to authorized individuals.

The following controls should be applied to the operation of the system as part of the validation process. These include:

- Limiting system access to authorized individuals
- Use of operational system checks
- Use of authority checks
- Use of device checks
- Determination that persons who develop, maintain, or use electronic systems have the education, training, and experience to perform their assigned tasks

---

14.   Ibid.
15.   Guidance for Industry, Title 21 CFR Part 11, "Electronic Records; Electronic Signatures—Scope and Application," U.S. Department of Health and Human Services, Food and Administration, Washington, D.C., August 2003.

■ Establishment of and adherence to written policies that hold individuals accountable for actions initiated under their electronic signatures
■ Appropriate controls over systems documentation
■ Controls for open systems[16] corresponding to controls for closed systems[17]
■ Requirements related to electronic signature

The second part of the approach is to create and maintain computer-generated, time-stamped audit trails to ensure the trustworthiness and reliability of the records. This should be part of a risk assessment of product quality, safety, and record integrity. Revision and change control should include maintaining copies of the original records. Device checks should be used to determine the validity of the source of data inputs or operational instructions.

The third part of the approach is a methodology for generating copies of records and correspondence. An auditor should have access to all of these documents. When electronic records are held in a common portable format they should be supplied in that format. In other cases, copies of the records should be converted to a common format such as PDF, XML, or SGML. If the organization has the ability to search, sort, or trend records, the copies should have the same capabilities. Finally, auditors should be able to inspect, review, and copy records in a human-readable form using the organization's hardware and following its established procedures and techniques for accessing records.

The final part covers record retention. Records should be accurate and readily retrievable throughout the retention period. Records can be archived in electronic format or nonelectronic media such as microfilm, microfiche, paper, or standard electronic formats. Copies should preserve the content and meaning of archived originals. Paper and electronic copies can co-exist as long as the content and meaning are preserved.

4.12 AN IT CASE STUDY

Wes Rhea, information security officer at a provider of specialized health management services and professor at Kennesaw State University, provided a case study

---

16.   Open system means an environment in which system access is not controlled by persons who are responsible for the content of electronic records that are on the system, ibid, 21CFR11.3, Definitions.
17.   Closed system means an environment in which system access is controlled by persons who are responsible for the content of electronic records that are on the system, ibid, 21CFR11.3, Definitions.

of information technology management. The organization has eight locations and employs approximately 6,000 persons.

Wes described how the organization supports SCM, BCP, SOX compliance, information security, and data protection. He also provided an example of a data center consolidation. See appendix B for a full description.

4.13 SUMMARY OF CHAPTER 4

This chapter described the importance of information technology. All major business systems rely on effective IT systems. This includes transaction systems such as SCM, ERP, and BCP.

IT plays an important role in compliance to SOX. IT directly supports nine sections in the act. This is especially true of the support required to effectively satisfy section 404, which requires an effective system of internal control and the associated sets of supporting controls.

Finally, there was a review of information security and the management of the IT control system. The ISO 27000 series of standards describes the methodology and management system processes used to assure an effective system of information security and CobIT describes an effective tool for managing IT risk and controls. The last element described was control of electronic records and electronic signatures provides described in FDA Title 21 CFR Part 11.

4.14 CHAPTER 4 EXERCISES

The following are the most common IT risks. Which ones apply to your organization?

■ Information security:
  • Uncontrolled systems access
  • Lack of an overlying security strategy
  • Decentralized or loosely organized security functions
  • Unusual facilities or business operations

■ Information systems strategy and planning:
  • Unmeasurable progress against plan
  • Outdated or nonexistent strategy
  • Impractical or unachievable strategies and plans

■ Database implementation and support:
  • Financial misstatement
  • Data corruption

■ Continuity planning:
  • Data loss
  • Disruption of operations
  • Direct expense of damages

■ Information systems operations:
  • Lack of training
  • No follow-up on errors or irregularities
  • Unsupportive management

■ Application system implementation and maintenance:
  • Cost overruns
  • Schedule overruns
  • Unsatisfactory functionality

■ Business process controls testing:
  • Data integrity
  • Transaction processing

- Application configuration
- Security
- Reporting

■ Network support:
  - Damaging exposure of critical systems
  - Costly downtime
  - Reduced productivity
  - Uncontrolled access to sensitive data

■ Systems software support:
  - Complexity of code
  - Unsafe programming languages
  - Lack of extensibility
  - Poor connectivity

■ Hardware support:
  - Downtime
  - Poor performance
  - Lack of vendor support
  - Lack of trained internal support

Chapter 5

Linking Lean Six Sigma to Management Systems and Information Technology

5.1 INTRODUCTION

Lean and Six Sigma are aimed at improving the quality of an organization's operations and improving its results. Both concentrate on customer satisfaction and improved business performance. Lean's focus is on time and waste reduction and improved throughput, while Six Sigma concentrates on reducing cost and increasing profits by eliminating variability, defects, and waste. It was natural to combine these programs because of the large amount of synergy between their goals and activities.

In this chapter we look at how Lean Six Sigma (LSS) links to financial management, ISO 9001 and ISO 14001, and information technology (IT). The projects implemented as part of an LSS program generate value to the customer and to the organization. However, they cannot operate in a vacuum. They require effective financial, quality, environmental, and other management systems. On the other hand, these management systems can be greatly improved by using LSS to provide valuable changes, which, if implemented correctly, result in positive effects to the organization's bottom line.

5.2 LEAN THINKING

Lean was developed by Fredrick Winslow Taylor, who used scientific management principles to improve assembly line manufacturing. This was later picked up by Henry Ford in manufacturing Ford Motor Co.'s automobiles. Taiichi Ohno expanded the philosophy and used it to establish the Toyota Production System. His processes are now used extensively all over the world.

The goals of lean are to satisfy internal and external customers while reducing time and waste. Waste is defined as anything that doesn't add value to the customer or increases cost to the organization. By reducing nonvalue-added activities, the processes are quicker, more effective, and costs are reduced.

Authors James P. Womack and Daniel T. Jones cite five principles of lean[1] as:

1. *"Provide value actually desired by the customers."* Value is defined by customer, created by the producer, and is what customers are willing to pay for. This is the defining concept of lean: adding value or decreasing nonvalue-added actions. Most companies waste 70 to 90 percent of their resources. Even the best waste 30 percent.

2. *"Identify the value stream for each product."* These are actions required to bring product or service to the customer.

3. *"Line up the remaining steps in a continuous flow."* This results in effective and efficient movement of product and/or services, information, and knowledge.

4. *"Let the customer pull value from the firm."* The downstream customer triggers the need for the product or service.

5. *"Start over in an endless search for perfection."* Perfection means no errors, no defects, and no waste.

5.2.1 Waste

There are eight types of waste[2] in lean: excess movement, excess inventory, wasted motion, delays in production, overproduction, overprocessing, poor-quality costs, and underutilization of personnel.

Waste 1: Excess movement. This consists of unnecessary movement of product. An example of this waste occurs when a product that's created on manufacturing line one is moved to line two to be completed. Lean can improve how a product moves in the plant, to distribution centers, or to the customer. It can also improve packing and loading of material during the shipping process. The result can be a reduction in labor costs, use of required equipment, and production costs.

Waste 2: Excess inventory. Inventory consists of raw materials, parts, in-process goods, or finished products. Excess inventory may be due to uncertain demand, poor product quality, or customer delivery delays. Major inventory costs are floor and warehouse space, equipment storage, labor, and cost of products or compo-

1. James P. Womack and Daniel T. Jones, *Lean Solutions* (Free Press, 2005), page 2.
2. George Alukal, "Create a Lean Mean Machine," *Quality Progress*, April 2003, pages 29–35.

nents held. Lean can be used to increase the number of inventory turns and reduce the cost of storage. An inventory turn is a full replenishment of stock.

Waste 3: Wasted motion. This consists of unnecessary movement of people during production, which results in more time to complete tasks and a waste of resources. An example is parts or tools that are too far from an operator. As a second example, if information on a product comes in on one computer and then the engineer has to input it to a second computer, the effort to transfer the information is wasted motion. This waste reduces the efficiency of personnel and increases costs.

Waste 4: Delays in production. This may be due to waiting for raw materials or parts to arrive, delayed staff assignments, or because of personnel absenteeism. Waiting results in idleness. A good example is a purchasing agent waiting for approvals to order materials. Another example is waiting for the completion of production meetings before starting production. The resultant loss of productivity can be very costly.

Waste 5: Overproduction. When an organization produces more product than it needs, it wastes materials, time, money, and labor. Overproduction is often the result of product defects or poor planning. This waste often results in excess inventory.

Waste 6: Overprocessing. This is due to performing unnecessary or incorrect steps in the production process, resulting in waste of personnel and materials. The end result is often a delay in product shipment. A prime example is an excessive number of approvals to make a product change.

Waste 7: Poor-quality costs. There are a number of poor-quality costs that can be reduced by lean. Examples are scrap, product or service defects, sorting, rework, and retesting. Poor quality results in time and money spent to correct mistakes, fix production problems, eliminate errors and defects, and retesting of repaired products. Three resulting costs are delays in shipment, increased production time, and use of additional production resources.

Waste 8: Underutilization of personnel. This occurs when the organization doesn't fully use its employees' experience, skills, knowledge, or ideas. This also occurs when personnel are placed in jobs without the correct training, which may be due to poorly defined competency requirements. As an example, if an individual is trained as an auditor but never assigned to an internal audit team, the training is a waste of resources.

An effective lean system identifies these sources of waste and provides methods to minimize them. The results are reduced cost and faster movement of product or service to the customer.

5.2.2 Lean tools

There are a large number of tools used in lean management. A key tool is value stream mapping, which maps a product or service from its supplier through the company to the customer. It can include information flow, time scale, and value-added designations. A key measure is the value-to-waste ratio. When starting waste management, most companies have a ratio of 5 to 10 percent. The goal for lean-enabled companies is 40 to 50 percent.

A value stream map can be used to identify opportunities for improvement. Nonvalue-added activities can be eliminated or simplified, even if they're not eliminated. After identifying waste, the value stream can then be translated into a desired-state map.

Another key tool is the balanced scorecard, which is often used to monitor the strategy of the organization. The first step is to determine strategic objectives. The objectives are often placed into four categories or perspectives: financial, customer, internal, and learning/growth.[3] These should be measurable and the data gathered analyzed to determine how well the objectives are being met. Some organizations develop an index from a weighted sum of the data.

5S is a methodology[4] used to create an efficient and safe workplace. It consists of the following activities:

- *Sort.* Separate necessary from unnecessary parts, tools, and supplies.
- *Set in order.* Neatly arrange and identify parts.
- *Shine.* Clean the work environment.
- *Standardize.* Conduct sort, set in order, and shine on a regular basis.
- *Sustain.* Integrate the 5S processes into the quality management system (QMS) and audit to ensure compliance.

Some organizations use the "5S + 1" methodology, which consists of the 5S activities, plus safety. Figure 5.1[5] lists some other common lean tools.

---

3. Robert S. Kaplan and David P. Norton, *The Balanced Scorecard* (Harvard Business School Press, 1996).
4. For a basic description of 5S methodology and other lean tools see Jay Arthur's *Lean Six Sigma Demystified* (McGraw-Hill, 2007).
5. Thomas Pyzdek, *The Six Sigma Handbook* (McGraw-Hill, 2003).

Figure 5.1	Common Lean Tools
Lean tool	**Use**
Plan-do-check-act (PDCA)	Continual improvement of processes.
Kaizen	Continual improvement of all activities of a business.
Kaizen events	Specific events resulting in targeted improvements.
Supplier, input, process, output, customer (SIPOC)	Provides a high-level map of customer-supplier process.
Visual communication	Replace words with pictures.
Just-in-time supply	Reduce inventory and lost time.
Jidoka	Operators can stop a process when problems occur.
One-piece flow	Reduce inventory and waiting time.

5.3 SIX SIGMA

Six Sigma is designed to reduce costs and increase profits by eliminating variability, defects, and waste. It was originally developed to improve manufacturing processes and eliminate defects. More recently, it has been extended to other types of business activities. In Six Sigma, a defect is defined as a failure to meet requirements.

Six Sigma was developed by Motorola in the mid-1980s to link the many tools of total quality management (TQM). Jack Welch of General Electric expanded on the program to effectively improve the bottom-line financials of the company. Other companies that were early users of Six Sigma are AlliedSignal and Honeywell.

In the Six Sigma philosophy, all work is a process and all processes have variability. Six Sigma focuses on customer satisfaction and improved business performance. The data gathered must be related directly or indirectly to customer needs and expectations. The data are then analyzed and turned into statistical information used to reduce process variability.

The Six Sigma metric goal is defined as 3.4 defects per million opportunities. Figure 5.2[6] shows the sigma levels from 2 to 6, the corresponding defect levels, and the cost of quality. Typical processes are at a three or four sigma level with cost of quality ranging from 13 to 40 percent of sales.

---

6. Robert M. Meisel, Steven J. Babb, Steven F. Marsh, and James P. Schlichting, *The Executive Guide to Understanding and Implementing Lean Six Sigma: The Financial Impact* (ASQ Quality Press, 2007).

Figure 5.2	Calculating Sigma	
Sigma level	**Defects per million opportunities**	**Cost of quality (% of sales)**
2	308,770	> 40%
3	66,807	25 – 40%
4	6,210	13 – 25%
5	233	5– 15%
6	3.4	< 5%

Cost of quality consists of four categories: prevention, appraisal, internal failure, and external failure.[7] Specific cost drivers are scrap, rework, returns, and complaints. Six Sigma works by reducing the defects and variability, which are major drivers of these costs.

5.3.1 Six Sigma methodology

The first activity of a Six Sigma effort is to identify the right project. Consider using a four-step project balanced scorecard to do this. Michael George defines a four-step project balanced scorecard.[8] The four steps are: corporate strategy, financial analysis, listening to the voice of the customer, and analysis of core processes. The project selected from the list of candidates should have the largest effect on the organization's bottom line.

The define-measure-analyze-improve-control (DMAIC) methodology is used on a project-by-project basis to improve the operation of the activities defined within a project. DMAIC is similar to the plan-do-check-act (PDCA) cycle. It takes the project from the definition stage through data gathering and analysis to the improve stage and finally through a continual improvement process. Figure 5.3 is a pictorial representation of DMAIC in terms of PDCA.

In the define stage, the project charter is created and the project team formed. The sponsoring organization must approve the definition, scope, and plans for the next stage.

The measure stage is used to gather data for determining current performance levels of the improvement activity. The data are analyzed to assure that the meas-

---

7. Jack Campanella, *Principles of Quality Costs, Principles, Implementation and Use*, Third Edition (ASQ Quality Press, 2005).
8. Michael L. George, *Lean Six Sigma: Combining Six-Sigma Quality with Lean Speed* (McGraw-Hill, 2002).

Figure 5.3 DMAIC and PDCA

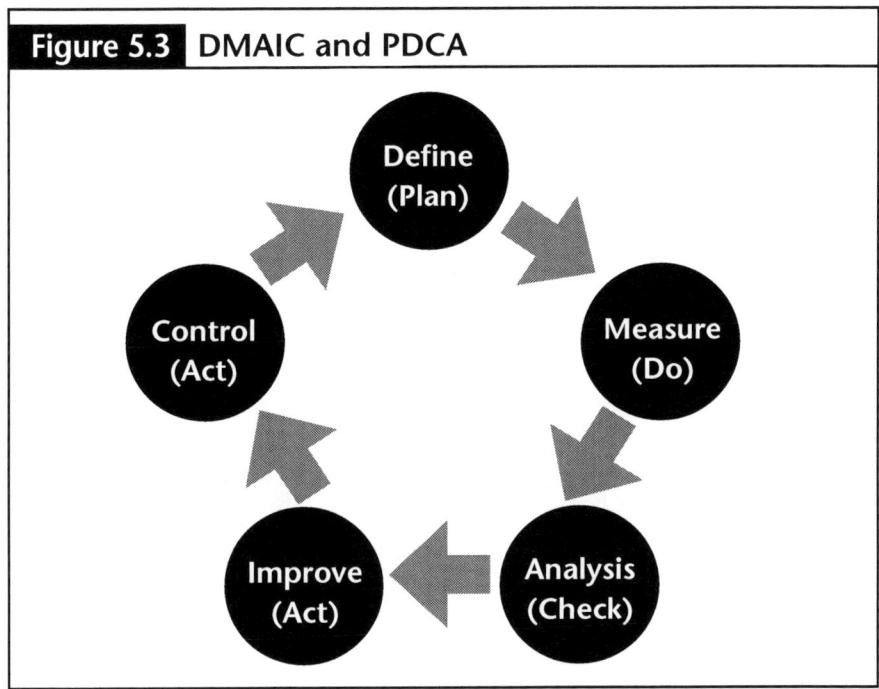

urements are accurate at the Six Sigma level. Again, the sponsoring organization must approve the selected data.

In the analyze stage, the team investigates the causes of variability. Potential causes include limited capabilities of personnel, processes, measurements, equipment, and the environment. There are many analysis tools that could be used in the analyze phase. These include cause-and-effect (Ishikawa or fishbone) diagrams, design of experiments (DOE), failure mode and effects analysis (FMEA), Pareto charts, and analysis of variance (ANOVA). This stage may also employ statistical quality control tools, such as control charts and process capability analysis. At the end of the analyze phase, the sponsoring organization will want to know what the team has learned about the relationship between inputs and outputs and what needs to be improved.

The improve stage is used to create lasting process changes. Its goals are to determine the major causes of variability and to correct them. The results should be that the products or services will be better, operate faster, and be cheaper to create. The team should listen to the customer and determine critical-to-quality (CTQ) measurements. The first step in this stage is to create a small-scale implementation project and gather data. The data are then analyzed and improvements identified. Many of the tools used in the analyze phase are also used in the improve phase. The team should develop balanced scorecards with measurements that typically cover the financials, customer satisfaction, quality, and continual improvement. The sponsoring organization will want to know the measurements taken, the results of the analysis, and the changes suggested by the team.

The final stage of the DMAIC process is control. A control plan is developed and used to implement the changes identified during the improve stage. Inputs and outputs are monitored and the variation in the product or service characteristics is driven toward the Six Sigma level.

Once the desired level is reached, the process is handed off to the sponsoring organization. The new procedures are documented and data collected on a continuing basis. Procedures are instituted to quickly identify variability and defects. The revised process may result in personnel changes and the need for training. As a final step, the team should review the entire project and develop lessons learned.

The power of DMAIC is that it starts with the voice of the customer, identifies statistical tools that have been around for years as part of TQM, and organizes them into an effective process for improvement. The end result is a cost-effective, stable process that satisfies customer needs. Note that DMAIC may incorporate some of the lean tools described earlier.

5.3.2 Design for Six Sigma

Design for Six Sigma (DFSS) evolved from DMAIC. It describes an effective process for creating new designs and consists of five stages: define, measure, analyze, design, and verify (DMADV).

The define stage starts with the creation of a cross-functional design team. The team defines the project goals and plans for the five phases. The key during this stage is to listen to the voice of the customer (VOC). This includes both internal and external customers. The team must identify risks associated with the project. At the end of this stage the team should have a solid charter that includes the business case.

The measure stage starts with the voice of the external and internal customers. The team needs to understand what external customers want in terms of products and services. These are defined as CTQ measurements. The team must also communicate with internal customers: sales, manufacturing, service, repair, and supply. At the completion of this stage, top management should feel that the VOC is well understood. There should also be a clear set of design requirements and CTQ measurements.

During the analyze stage, the team must define and evaluate a high-level process design. The team will use a number of tools during this stage. It usually starts with brainstorming sessions to define the initial design followed by a functional analysis of the design. CTQ measures are key elements of the analysis. Another tool often used is quality function deployment (QFD), which links the product or service functions to the design requirements. The team must also identify potential suppliers and determine the support required of information technology personnel. At the end of this stage, the team reviews the proposed new design with managers to demonstrate how it satisfies the VOC.

The goal of the design stage is to create and evaluate a detailed design. The team performs a value-added analysis to determine the activities that add value and those that do not. This analysis is used with other tools to optimize the design performance. Two tools commonly used in this stage are mistake proofing (*poka-yoke*), and design of experiments (DOE). The design is generally reviewed twice, halfway through this stage and at the end.

The verify stage starts with development of a pilot system. After the pilot run, the results are analyzed. The learning and feedback from the pilot step are crucial to the development of the product or service. Quality management, product testing, quality control procedures, and field service are developed during the pilot stage. After the completion of the pilot, a management review is held to assure completion of the design process. The organization can then start production.

5.3.3 Six Sigma tools

Figure 5.4 lists common Six Sigma tools and their uses.

5.3.4 Key Six Sigma personnel

One of Six Sigma's biggest strengths is its strong definition of roles for key personnel. Figure 5.5 on page 91 contains a list of the key Six Sigma personnel and their functions. A team usually includes a leader who may be a Champion, a Black Belt or a Green Belt, a facilitator, and subject matter experts. Also often attached to the team are a management/executive sponsor, the process owner, and a financial expert.

Figure 5.4 Common Six Sigma Tools	
Six Sigma tool	**Use**
Quality function deployment (house of quality)	Transform customer requirements into the product design.
Design for X	Develop processes for activities such as manufacture, assembly, test, reliability, etc.
Critical-to-quality measures	Understand what is important to the customer.
Poka-yoke	Mistake proofing
Design of experiments	A statistical tool used to determine relationships between a set of variables.
Hypothesis testing	A statistical methodology for making decisions based on data.
Regression analysis	A statistical method for determining the relationship between independent variables and dependent variables.
Failure mode and effects analysis	A method to determine potential failures and their effects.
TRIZ	The theory of innovative problem solving

5.4 LINKING LEAN SIX SIGMA TO FINANCIAL MANAGEMENT

Lean Six Sigma's (LSS) goal is to reduce the cost of operations and add value to the organization's bottom line. In chapter 1 we defined the financial management system as consisting of six elements: investment management, statement of cash flow, profit-and-loss (P&L) statement, the balance sheet, the general ledger, and a system of internal control. Although LSS can contribute to each of these items, its major contributions are to the P&L statement and the balance sheet.

LSS contributes to the P&L statement by improving net profits. Profits are improved by increasing revenues through improved customer satisfaction. LSS can improve product throughput by creating a more efficient manufacturing or service process. This can be done by reducing the eight wastes defined in section 5.2.1.

LSS also can decrease overhead by reducing the cost of goods sold (COGS), which includes the quality of the products and services, the cost of purchased materials, and operating and production costs. Reducing the eight wastes defined

Figure 5.5 | Key Six Sigma Personnel

Key Six Sigma personnel	Function
Management/executive sponsors	Upper-level managers who create and drive the effort. They create the strategic plans, business plans, and work on strategic policy deployment. They also create a list of projects and communicate to staff about them.
Champions	Responsible for project implementation. They assign Black and Green Belts to projects, communicate successes, and reward and recognize teams.
Process owners	Responsible for process to be improved.
Master Black Belts	Experts on Six Sigma. They are the trainers and coaches and lead major projects.
Black Belts	Lead projects and are known as change agents. They get four to twelve weeks of training.
Green Belts	Support Black Belts. Similar training to Black Belts. May be part time.
Team members	Subject matter experts. May be part time on a project.
Financial analysts	Define potential savings during define phase. Document project results including financial gains. Monitor success twelve months after project completion.

in section 5.2.1 can significantly improve the expense line. Six Sigma's goal of reducing defect levels will result in lower costs and improved customer satisfaction. LSS can be used to eliminate nonvalue-added activities and improve the efficiency of the organization's processes. LSS can also be used to decrease transaction costs and optimize organizational efficiency.

LSS can contribute to improving the balance sheet by reducing the cash tied up in inventory or reducing the spending of capital. The reduction in nonvalue-added activities can improve efficiency and eliminate the need to hire additional help. LSS can also have intangible benefits, such as increased customer satisfaction, increased employee satisfaction, and increased workplace safety.

5.4.1 Lean Six Sigma success stories

Michael George[9] provides two success stories that are very instructive. In the first example, he describes a manufacturer that had an overloaded production schedule because of increased orders. The order-entry process was complex and the organization was concerned about customer retention, as customer satisfaction was poor.

The team responsible for solving the problem mapped the flow of activities, which found many nonvalue-added steps. It categorized activities as value-added, nonvalue-added, steps that could be reduced, and steps that could be moved.

The results were a reduction in the number of steps from twenty-one to seven. The company did not have to add personnel to handle the greater load, process lead time was reduced by 72 percent, cycle efficiency increased from 7 percent to 22 percent, and savings amounted to $240,000 per year.

In the second example, George described a company that was doing a poor job of responding to customer inquiries. It was losing customers because of an inability to respond quickly to complaints. One option was to hire more staff.

The LSS team created a three-phased value stream map of the process. In phase one, sales received the customer input and requests information from production control. Phase two consisted of production control responding to sales. In phase three, sales responded to the customer. The problem was that phase one was being overwhelmed by a large number of low-priority requests.

The fix consisted of dedicating sales reps to handle requests that needed to be expedited. The organization also improved the hand-off process and provided training in the expediting process. The results were a reduction in average handling time from 5.8 days to 1.5 days. The incremental sales and labor savings resulted in an increase in operating income of $147,000.

As another example, the Naval Surface Warfare Center's Indian Head Division initiated an LSS program in 2004 after other improvement programs failed. Naval personnel at the center manufacture war materials for fighters, including propellant mixtures, rockets, mines, undersea weapons, and ship-mounted guns. From 2005 to 2007, the organization saved $8.9 million as a result of its LSS efforts,[10] which included:

---

9.   Michael L. George, *Lean Six Sigma: Combining Six Sigma Quality with Lean Speed* (McGraw-Hill, 2002).

10.   Terry Widner and Mitch Gallant, "A Launch to Quality," *Quality Progress*, February 2008, 38–43.

- Reduced vendor certification time by 1,000 hours
- Reduced the time needed to process travel orders by 183 hours
- Created a utilities algorithm that saved $584,000
- Created real-time X-rays and digital X-raying of the Zuni rocket that reduced labor by 5,000 hours and saved about $300,000 in material requirements

Honeywell International has also had a great deal of success with LSS. From 1994 to 2002, Honeywell exceeded $3 billion in financial benefits from its program.[11] At one of its chemical plants in Europe, a Honeywell LSS team used design of experiments and process flow simplification to turn a $900,000 loss into a $3.4 million gain.

5.5 LSS, ISO 9001, AND ISO 14001

For LSS to be effective in the long term, an organization must have an efficient quality management system (QMS) and environmental management system (EMS). For this book, we will use ISO 9001 and ISO 14001 as the basis for QMS and EMS.

5.5.1 DMAIC, ISO 9001 and ISO 14001

The define phase of DMAIC is used to create the project purpose, scope, and scale. The team is also created during this element and may contain the following positions: sponsor, Black Belt, Green Belt, and other members. The organization and team use the VOC to determine customer requirements.

The following planning clauses of ISO 9001 relate to the define phase.

- Clause 7.1, Planning of product realization, requires planning and the development of processes needed for product realization. This consists of defining quality objectives and requirements; developing verification, validation, monitoring, inspection, and test activities; acceptance criteria; and records needed.
- Clause 7.2.1 requires the organization to determine customer requirements, clause 7.2.2 requires it to review the requirements related to the product, and clause 7.2.3 requires a means of communicating with the customer.
- Clause 7.5.1, Control of production and service provision, describes methods for planning and performing production. This includes requirements for

---

11. William J Hill and Willie Kearney, "The Honeywell Experience," *Six Sigma Magazine*, February 2003, 34–37.

product information; work instructions; availability of suitable equipment, including monitoring and measuring devices; and defining release, delivery, and post-delivery activities.

The relevant ISO 14001 clause is 4.4.6, Operational control, which requires creating procedures to identify significant environmental aspects and communicating applicable procedures and requirements to suppliers.

The measure phase of DMAIC is used to create a baseline for determining current performance of a product or service. The data-gathering method for the process is identified during the measure element. ISO 9001 has three clauses relating to data gathering: clause 8.2.3, Monitoring and measurement of processes; clause 8.2.4, Monitoring and measurement of product; and clause 8.2.1, Customer satisfaction measurements. The relevant ISO 14001 clause is 4.5.1, which requires procedures to monitor and measure operations that can have significant environmental impacts.

Sources of variation are investigated during the analyze phase. This phase starts with historical data, but then focuses on gathering new data. It's important to look for root causes of variability. The relevant ISO 9001 clause is 8.4, Analysis of data, which requires data analysis to assure conformity to product requirements, characteristics, and trends of processes and products; opportunities for preventive action; and supplier data. The relevant ISO 14001 clause is 4.5.2, which requires evaluation of compliance to legal and other requirements.

The next DMAIC phase is improve, which creates lasting process improvements. The team needs to decide on the potential root causes to improve and how to counter the effects of these causes. This phase includes a small-scale pilot implementation. The ISO 9001 clauses that are relevant to the improve phase are 8.5.1, Continual improvement; 8.5.2, Corrective action; and 8.5.3, Preventive action. The relevant ISO 14001 clause is 4.5.3, which requires identification of nonconformities and corrective and preventive actions.

The final DMAIC phase is control. During this phase, implemented solutions are evaluated and their improvements maintained. The organization maintains control of the inputs and monitors outputs with the goal of reducing variation. A methodology is developed to provide early warning about potential problems. The organization documents new procedures, sets up data-collection processes, and implements ongoing monitoring processes. During this phase, the team determines lessons learned and passes the information on to the rest of the organization.

The ISO 9001 clause that supports the control phase is 5.6, Management review. This clause requires determining the status of the QMS. Subclauses 5.6.2, Review inputs; and 5.6.3, Review outputs, provide details of this review. Clause 5.6.2 requires a review of the results of audits, customer feedback, process performance, and product conformity, status of preventive and corrective actions, and follow-up of actions from previous management reviews. Clause 5.6.3, Review outputs, requires decisions and actions to improve processes, improve processes related to customer requirements, and new resource needs. The corresponding ISO 14001 clause is 4.6, Management review, which contains input and output requirements similar to ISO 9001's clause 5.6.

5.5.2 DFSS, ISO 9001, and ISO 14001

There is a great deal of similarity between the way ISO 9001 and ISO 14001 work with DMAIC and how they work with DFSS. Figure 5.6 shows the relationship between DFSS process to the define-measure-analyze-design-verify (DMADV) process.

5.6 LEAN SIX SIGMA AND INFORMATION TECHNOLOGY

A major link between LSS and information technology (IT) is project management. The software used by organizations may have been developed for general projects within an organization, but LSS will require special software because of the vast array of LSS tools and the need to keep track of success stories, especially those showing financial gains from the projects.

Software is also needed to show the connections to the customers and the suppliers of the organizations' products or services. An effective LSS project must show an understanding of the VOC and communications between the design team and suppliers. There is a strong need to capture events as part of the project's history, including periodic reviews of progress.

Database and program availability need to be straightforward so that the LSS team can effectively pursue the goals of the project. This is especially important for workers at remote locations or those who work from home.

Many of the tools used in LSS require a great deal of computation and logical decision making. Some are very sophisticated with software programs required for effective operation. Because of this, there is a strong connection between LSS and IT.

Figure 5.6	The Relationships between ISO 9001 and ISO 14001 and DMADV	
DFSS element	**ISO 9001 clause**	**ISO 14001 clause**
Define: Listen to the customer.	7.2.1: Determine product related requirements 7.2.2: Review the requirements 7.2.3: Communicate with the customer 7.3.1: Design-and-development planning 7.3.2: Design-and-development inputs	4.3.1: Identify environmental aspects 4.3.2: Identify legal and other requirements 4.4.3: Communication 4.3.2.2: Agreement with customers 4.4.6a: Documented procedures 4.4.6c: Identify significant environmental aspects.
Measure: Determine critical-to-quality measures.	7.3.3: Design-and-development outputs	4.4.6.c: Operational control: Identify significant environmental aspects.
Analyze: Determine and evaluate the high level design.	7.3.4: Design-and-development review: Identify problems and corrective actions.	4.4.6.a: Operational control: Identify control situations that could lead to environmental deviations.
Design: Create, evaluate, verify, and optimize the design.	7.3.5: Design-and-development verification	4.4.6: Operational control: Ensure significant environmental aspects are performed under specified conditions.
Verify: Create, run, and analyze a pilot; start production; test in service; provide field service.	7.3.6: Design-and-development validation 7.3.7: Control design and development changes.	4.4.6: Operational control: Identify and plan operations.

The automation of these tools, as well as the management systems that use them, require software professionals with a strong background in statistical analysis and program management. They must understand the fundamentals of LSS. The basic goals of LSS are a simplification of processes by removing nonvalue-added activities and a reduction in variability and defectives during operations. Software developers need to keep these in mind when developing the LSS software. Of equal importance is the need to simplify the organization's processes before handing them over to the software developers.

The LSS philosophy can have a positive effect on software development. In fact, the DMADV or DMAIC philosophies are often applied to develop new software or re-engineer old software. The development of LSS software will go through the same stages as any other software development. At the start of the project the error rate will be high as problem conditions are identified. As fixes are applied, new problems will arise. This is where application of DMADV or DMAIC can result in superior software.

For example, look at the basic cash flow process in a company. Transaction management requires accurate purchase orders, fast information flow, and low management cost. IT is not only used to manage transactions, but the system can also generate a useful amount of data. This data can then be used as inputs to a host of automated LSS tools.

5.7 LSS SOFTWARE

There are two types of software used to support LSS: analytical tools, which are used to perform statistical or process analysis, and program management tools, which are used to track the LSS program and projects.

One of the leading providers of software tools used in LSS is Minitab. Minitab's software manages data, transforms them into specified formats and statistical studies such as regression, DOE, and ANOVA. It can also perform behavior analysis (statistical process control), measurements system analysis, reliability/survival analysis, multivariate analysis, graph data, and generate reports.[12]

Another useful software package is Visio. This is a diagramming and flowchart software tool used with Microsoft Windows. It uses vector graphics to create diagrams and work flows. Visio comes in two packages: standard and professional. They share the same interface, though the professional edition has added templates and layouts that make it easier for users to connect diagrams to data sources and to display data graphically.

5.8 TWO CASE STUDIES

Case study 5.1 describes a DMAIC project at a warehouse in New Jersey. It is an example of directly linking quality and financial management using a Six Sigma technique. The DMAIC technique is used to directly improve the inventory proc-

---

12. *www.minitab.co/products/minitab/features*

ess at the warehouse and reduce cost of operations resulting in a gain of the profit margin.

The second case study was provided by the Juran Institute Inc. It describes a success story linking Six Sigma to financial management. It uses the DMADV technique to redesign a tool used by resellers to quote projects that use the company's products. Both case studies are good examples of how quality can link to financial management and improve bottom-line results.

5.9 SUMMARY OF LINKING LEAN SIX SIGMA

LSS is a powerful program for improving the bottom-line of a company in addition to providing value to its customers. Lean engineering seeks out the voice of the customer and then focuses on customer satisfaction while improving the speed of operations and reducing waste. Six Sigma determines the causes of defects and focuses on eliminating process variability.

This chapter described how LSS links to financial, quality, and environmental management systems. We saw that information technology is an essential support for LSS processes and tools. The major goals of LSS are customer satisfaction and improvement of the organization's bottom line. LSS has a successful track record in satisfying both.

5.10 CHAPTER 5 EXERCISES

How does LSS contribute to the management systems in your organization? Identify at least two LSS projects in your organization that supported (a) financial management, (b) quality management and/or environmental management and (c) information technology.

- Who were the members of the LSS teams in each project?
- What were the major improvements obtained by each project?
- What were the financial gains for each project?

Chapter 6

Implementing Linked Management Systems

6.1 INTRODUCTION

The methodology for linking management systems consists of three major elements: a system of internal control, a risk-based set of controls, and a linked auditing system.

Chapter 2 discussed quality management system (QMS) and environmental management system (EMS) support of the system of internal control required by the Sarbanes-Oxley Act (SOX). The most common system of internal control is based on the guidance from the Committee of Sponsoring Organizations of the Treadway Commission (COSO). Some of the material from chapter 2 will be repeated to make the current discussion coherent.

Next, we will look at the controls used by financial, quality, and environmental management and put them in the context of risk management. Financial controls are used to ensure the accuracy of financial statements. Quality and environmental management controls are related to the "shall" statements in the two systems and are used to ensure compliance to ISO 9001 and ISO 14001. In both cases, internal auditing must test these controls and provide an opinion concerning the effectiveness of the management systems.

A linked or integrated internal auditing system is essential for understanding the status of the overall management system. We will look at the structure of such a system and indicate what management must do to ensure its effectiveness.

Finally, we will describe a methodology for implementing a linked management system.

6.2 QMS/EMS SUPPORT OF A SYSTEM OF INTERNAL CONTROL

SOX mandates a system of internal control to manage risk in the organization. A system published by COSO in 1992[1] provides the basis for internal controls used by many organizations. This system is the foundation for good governance that preceded SOX. There are five components of the COSO internal controls:

- Control environment
- Information and communication
- Risk assessment
- Monitoring
- Control activities

6.2.1 Control environment

The control environment (CE) is the foundation for all other COSO elements. This element looks at the "tone at the top" of the organization and determines whether it does things right and whether it does the right things. The CE also looks at integrity in the dealings of the organization, complaints of misconduct, and the competence of personnel.

The QMS provides strong inputs that help create the foundation for the rest of the COSO guidance. Chief among these is the process approach defined in ISO 9001's clause 4.1. The process approach requires definition of all processes; their sequence and interaction; availability of needed resources; and methods of monitoring, measuring, and analysis. The process approach can also be extended to financial management processes.

There are other ISO 9001 clauses that support the COSO foundation. These include definition of policy, objectives, and planning described in clauses 5.3, 5.4.1, 7.1, and 8.1. The requirements of demonstrating management commitment in clause 5.1 and internal communication in clause 5.5.3 support the ideal "tone at the top." Finally, clause 6.2.2 requires employee competence.

6.2.2 Information and communication

COSO requires capture and communication of internal and external information used by individuals to perform their responsibilities and to make informed

---

1. COSO: The Committee of Sponsoring Organizations of the Treadway Commission.

business decisions. The information should flow up, across, and down the organization. There should also be processes that address employee, supplier, and customer concerns in a timely manner.

ISO 9001 has clauses that cover control of documents (4.2.3), control of records (4.2.4), top management communication (5.1), and internal communication (5.5.3). With respect to customer and supplier communication, ISO 9001 clauses 7.2.1, 7.2.2, 7.2.3, and 7.4 define customer requirements, customer communication, purchasing, and supplier communication respectively. When these clauses are effectively in place they will help personnel conduct, manage, and control the organization's operations.

6.2.3 Risk assessment

Risk assessment starts with the definition of the organization's objectives and their risks. The objectives should be compatible. It's essential to determine which risks are critical and to formulate actions to mitigate them. It's also important to develop a methodology to deal with change and its associated risks. Risk management has much in common with the next COSO element, monitoring.

ISO 9001's support of the monitoring requirement starts with the definition of measurable objectives required by clause 5.4.1. The philosophy is that objectives must be measurable or improvement can't be measured. This means that data must be measured, analyzed, and turned into information. The next section covering the COSO monitoring requirement will discuss this in more detail. Suffice it to say, the data must be analyzed and turned into information in clause 8.4, which is then used in a continual improvement process (clause 8.5.1) and corrective and preventive actions (clauses 8.5.2 and 8.5.3). Finally, everything is tied together in management review (clause 5.6).

It should be noted that ISO 14001 covers many of the same requirements for environmental management. Clause 4.3.1 of ISO 14001 requires the definition of aspects that can have a significant effect on the environment. These aspects may impose a major risk to the organization.

6.2.4 Monitoring

Monitoring focuses on obtaining data about the operations of the organization and is closely related to risk assessment. Monitoring assesses the quality of the system's performance over separate evaluations and/or ongoing monitoring activities. It uses internal auditing, management and supervision of operations, and actions of personnel performing their duties. During auditing, auditors must drill down to the root causes of problems, follow audit trails, and identify significant deficiencies and material weaknesses. The resultant data are analyzed and the information learned is fed into the risk-assessment process.

ISO 9001 can provide data from many sources. There is the continual monitoring and measuring of products and processes required by clauses 8.2.3 and 8.2.4. There are also requirements to gather customer satisfaction data (clause 8.2.1) and to conduct internal audits (clause 8.2.2). Other data that are available consist of contract review (clause 7.2) and supplier data (clause 7.4.3). The data must be analyzed in clause 8.4 and turned into information in the continual improvement clause (8.5.1).

6.2.5 Control activities

Control activities are the policies and procedures that help ensure that management directives are followed. They ensure that timely actions are taken to address risks to the organization's objectives. They cover exceptions to policy and information that requires follow up. A key control activity is the timely actions taken to mitigate risks to the organization's objectives. Control activities monitor significant plans and programs, such as the management of supplier products and outsourced services.

ISO 9001 and ISO 14001 provide a great deal of support to COSO's required control activities. Both standards contain requirements for corrective and preventive action (ISO 9001 clauses 8.5.2 and 8.5.3, and ISO 14001 clause 4.5.3). These standards also require control of nonconforming product (ISO 9001 clause 8.3) and environmental nonconformities (ISO 14001 clause 4.5.3). Finally, ISO 14001 requires procedures for emergency preparedness and response (clause 4.4.7).

6.2.6 Linking ISO 9001 and ISO 14001 to COSO guidance

As you can see, there are a number of ISO 9001 and ISO 14001 clauses that support COSO. In addition, ISO 9001 requires a quality manual to document the management system. The link can be made in the manual or in a separate document. The manual can be extended to an organizational manual containing a description of how ISO 9001's and ISO 14001's requirements are satisfied and how they link to the COSO guidance. The links should be summarized in a separate section of the manual. In this way, the organization can provide auditors and staff with an understanding of the links. Auditors can look at clauses supporting COSO to verify that an effective system of internal control exists.

The manual should also contain a listing of the controls that can be used by management and auditors to ensure compliance to ISO 9001, ISO 14001, and the effective system of internal control required by SOX.

6.3 THE CONTROL ENVIRONMENT

6.3.1 What are controls?

A financial control is a process designed to provide assurance regarding the reliability of financial reporting and the preparation of financial statements. It should be prepared in accordance with generally accepted accounting principles (GAAP). Quality controls provide assurance that requirements of quality management standards are met.

Controls should provide reasonable assurance that transactions are properly recorded and provide prevention and/or timely detection of unauthorized acquisition or disposition of assets. A good control must include accurate maintenance of records and is a tool that can be used to identify risks.

A good internal control system as required by SOX section 404 ensures that financial statements are accurate and comply with accepted standards, that good records are kept, and that assets are employed as intended. The system must manage control breaks—whether financial, operational, or regulatory—that can lead to significant financial loss if not corrected in a timely manner. Preventive controls are designed to avoid a control break, while detective controls are designed to identify a break after it has occurred.

6.3.2 Types of controls

There are two types of controls used to provide evidence of compliance to SOX: entity-level and activity-level controls.

Entity-level controls apply throughout an organization and are often represented in the mission and value statements with an assessment of an organization's strengths, weaknesses, opportunities, and threats. They provide inputs to the organization's overall strategy. Some examples of entity-level controls are initiating, recording, processing, and reconciling account balances; processing of nonroutine transactions; prevention, identification, and detection of fraud; automated data validation and edit checks; limited access to confidential information; and transactions that are numbered prior to entry.

Activity-level controls focus on major business units or functions, such as sales, production, marketing, technology development, and research and development. Successfully assessing activity-level risks contributes to maintaining acceptable levels of risk at the entity level. Examples of activity-level controls are reconciliation of general ledger items to a subsidiary ledger, assurance that incoming material meets specifications, control of the manufacturing and service provisioning processes, accurate inventory control, assuring that shipped goods are accurately billed, and accurately recorded invoices for all authorized shipments.

Both types of controls have risks. Entity-level risks include external factors such as technology developments, competition, and new legislation. Internal factors that pose risks for entity-level controls are a disruption in information system processing, incompetence of personnel, changes in management responsibilities, and fraud.

Examples of activity-level risks are information not entered for materials received on a timely basis, lost receiving reports or shipping records, inadequate physical security, inadequate skilled labor, employee carelessness, and poor product or service quality.

Quality management controls consist of "shall" statements accompanied by a quality record and measurements that describe process performance. Examples from ISO 9001 include management review (clause 5.6.1), training records (clause 6.2.2), contract review requirements (clause 7.2.2), design-and-development inputs (clause 7.3.2), validation (clause 7.3.6), purchasing evaluations (clause 7.4.1), audit records (clause 8.2.2), corrective actions (clause 8.5.2), and preventive actions (clause 8.5.3).

There are also operational controls for the size and age of inventories, the supply of critical components, product shipping, product received from suppliers, and record retention. Important set of metrics relating to the supply chain consist of delivery performance, cycle time, inventory, cash management, and supply chain costs.

6.3.3 What are key controls?

Key controls are transactions that ensure the accuracy of financial statement assertions. There are two schools of thought regarding them. If the risk may prevent the satisfaction of financial assertions, then the controls that address the risk are identified as key controls. On the other hand, key controls assure that only valid transactions flow into significant accounts and are completely and accurately processed and recorded.

Key controls should be evaluated from the standpoints of design and operating effectiveness. Test the design to determine whether the design of the control may effectively prevent or detect misstatements of material accounts. Next, evaluate the operating effectiveness by testing examples to see whether the key control prevents or detects material misstatements.

6.3.4 Testing controls

Management ultimately determines the number of controls to be tested and the level of testing (frequency and sample size). Key controls and controls that are performed frequently should be tested to a greater extent. Four types of tests offer varying levels of assurance:

■ *Inquiry*: asking people if certain controls are in place and functioning
■ *Observation*: observing actual controls in operation
■ *Inspection*: reviewing evidence of a given control procedure
■ *Re-performance*: Repeating a given control procedure

Inquiry offers the lowest level of assurance; repeated performance offers the highest level of assurance.

Management should establish a multi-year review cycle for testing key internal controls. The testing should include reviewing all of the assessable units and significant accounts at least every three years.

Monitoring and ongoing risk assessment of internal controls should be conducted to determine the adequacy of design for proper execution and effectiveness. There are three types of monitoring activity: self-assessments, peer reviews, and internal audits. Internal audits are the most effective in determining the risk associated with controls. The results of the assessments should indicate design effectiveness, operating effectiveness, and control gaps. It's important to identify and test compensating controls[2] and to document test results.

The effectiveness of a control is affected by the directness of the control technique in relation to the major program or financial reporting process, the frequency of the control application, the experience and skills of personnel performing the control, and the procedures followed when a control identifies an exception condition.

To understand the design of a control consider the following questions:

■ Do the controls mitigate program risk to an acceptable level?

---

2. These separate duties that should not be combined in one position. For example, the person who approves a voucher should not write the check.

- How can a potential misstatement in significant financial reporting processes affect the related line item or account at the financial reporting assertion level?
- How do the related control objectives prevent or detect the potential misstatement?
- Are identified control techniques likely to help achieve the control objective?

Design effectiveness of a control is determined by reviewing the characteristics and documentation associated with the control, evaluating the design effectiveness by flowcharting and process mapping, and testing the design effectiveness by conducting interviews of key personnel and walkthroughs of major processes.

Operating effectiveness is determined by conducting interviews of key personnel and walkthroughs of major processes using actual data. An auditor should ask, "Are the controls functioning as designed?" Testing operating effectiveness includes reviewing supporting documentation for proper authorization, reviewing the results of periodic reconciliations, and reviewing the policy and procedure to determine if they are being followed. Sampling techniques may be used.

6.3.5 Control gaps

A control gap exists when a control for a given financial statement assertion doesn't exist, doesn't adequately address a relevant assertion, or isn't operating effectively. When management encounters a control gap, it should consider the extent of the gap, the effect it will have in the assurance statement, and whether compensating controls exist that mitigate the risk of misstatement. These controls should be identified and tested.

When a control gap is identified, it should be determined whether a compensating control is in place to mitigate the risk associated with the control gap. When a compensating control is in place, test the design and operating effectiveness in the same manner as for other controls.

6.3.6 Document test results

Documentation should be maintained that shows the evaluation of controls at the entity and activity levels and any deficiencies identified. Documentation should provide a clear understanding of the purpose of the control, the source of data, and the conclusions reached.

Documentation should be organized to provide a clear link to significant findings or reported weaknesses. The documentation must enable a knowledgeable person with no previous connection with the assessment to understand the nature, timing, extent, and results of the procedures performed, understand the evidence obtained, support the conclusions reached, and determine who performed the work and the date it was completed.

Management should consider implementing policies regarding documentation retention if such policies don't already exist, providing detailed instruction to the assessment team on the specific documents to be maintained and the format to assure consistency across the organization.

6.3.7 Ongoing monitoring and testing

A valuable tool used as part of the controls process is ongoing monitoring and testing. It provides an independent view of the management testing and assessment process and is used to advise management regarding the design, scope, and frequency of testing. Some of the functions provided are effectiveness testing, identification of control gaps, performing follow-up review of control gap fixes, and coordination between management and third-party auditors regarding scope and test plans.

Some examples of monitoring controls are shipping; receiving; inventory control; accounts payable; transaction processing; whether assets or liabilities exist at a given date; tests of whether asset, liability, equity, revenue, and expense components are included in the financial statements at appropriate amounts; and tests of IT controls.

6.3.8 Audit of a system of internal controls

A third-party auditor's testing agenda should be based on a top-down risk-based approach. The auditor should perform walkthroughs of key controls and run or review individual transactions to see if they were done correctly. Transactions should be picked randomly on different days to see that they were done correctly and that procedures were followed.

To satisfy SOX section 404(b), the external auditor must attest to the effectiveness of the system of internal control required each fiscal year. Material changes must be reported every quarter. The report must address the design and effectiveness of the system and provide proof of actual tests of the controls and the results of the tests. Quality management techniques can be used to provide continual improvement of the internal control system and its processes.

6.4 INTERNAL AUDITING

6.4.1 Auditing to add value

The main goal of internal audits is to provide top management and the board of directors with an accurate understanding of the organization's financial and operational status. Top management must certify that material financial and non-financial information are included in financial reports[3].

Combining QMS and EMS tools with the financial auditing function and procedures will result in more effective audits and increase the understanding of the material nonfinancial information of the organization. The changing internal financial auditing scope has moved away from compliance to regulations to adding value through operational effectiveness and risk management.

It should be noted that a major goal of internal audits is to improve the management systems. The audit team should be unbiased and without any conflict of interest with the processes or systems under audit.

Two of the many added values of ISO 9001 and ISO 14001 are the process approach and continual improvement. Many organizations extend the process approach to a set of process audits, which is an effective way of evaluating the status of an organization and managing its risks. Process audits are used to evaluate both the operational effectiveness of the organization and the financial management system.

6.4.2 The financial audit team's tasks

Figure 6.1 illustrates a financial audit team's tasks. The remainder of this section adds details for these tasks.

The controller should determine the financial risks to the organization based on five characteristics: the size of the major accounts, the number of transactions, risk as a percentage of revenue, the value of assets, and the likelihood of occurrence. The risk level matrix described in chapter 3 can be used to identify the biggest risks. The results may then be used to determine the internal control audit plan and checklists.

The auditors' work is focused on determining what to audit based on the controller's risk assessment. They must determine the "tone at the top" of the company by interviewing top management and using appropriate survey instruments.[4]

---

3. "Sarbanes-Oxley Section 404: A Guide for Management by Internal Control Practitioners," pg 22, The Institute of Internal Auditors, *www.theiia.org*

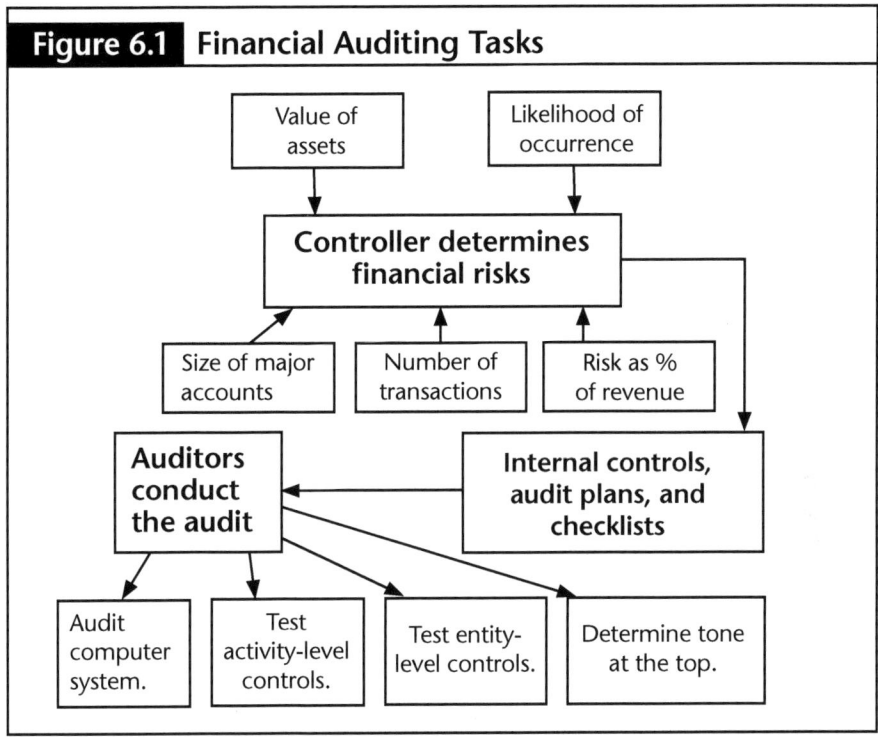

Figure 6.1 | **Financial Auditing Tasks**

The audit team determines how to perform tests of the entity-level and activity-level controls that will give an accurate picture of the procedures, processes, data analysis, and corrective actions.

Entity-level controls apply throughout the organization. Examples are human resource policies, codes of conduct, communication strategies, accounting policies, risk-assessment processes, and the organization's structure.

Activity-level controls apply in various parts of the organization. Examples are reconciliation[5] of general ledger entries to a subsidiary ledger, automated data validation and edit checks, paper-based information reviewed and approved prior to entry, validation of customer orders, testing whether shipped goods are accurately billed in the proper period, and testing invoices and accounts receivable for accuracy.

---

4. One common tool is *ALLTELL Control and Risk Self-Assessment Processes* (The Institute of Internal Auditors, 2005).
5. Reconciliation: The process of comparing information that exists in two systems or locations. Variances are analyzed and corrections made so that the information is accurate and consistent.

The team must also determine how to audit the information in the computer system and create an internal control audit plan and checklists. These must include the accounting and financial procedures and the information systems.

If the organization is process-based, the audit will consist of a set of individual process audits that cover the key functions used. Some specific audit questions to be considered by the team include:

■ Are the accounting and operations systems based on the risk analysis?
■ What is the "tone at the top" of the company?
■ What is the accuracy of the financial statements?
■ What is the accuracy of the information in the computer system?

The audit team will examine each process and procedure to determine the risks involved and ensure that responsibilities are correctly identified and duties are adequately separated. An example of separation of duties is: The person who validates a payment must not be the person who writes the check. The goal is to prevent fraud.

The audit team should test a sample of the processes and procedures. The testing process consists of randomly picking transactions for different days to see if they were done correctly. Then the team looks for triggers and the processes followed when the triggers occur. An alternate method of testing is to use a practice database or "sandbox" to print forms and reports which verify that transactions are done correctly. The "sandbox" can also be used to assure that data are stored correctly.

Finally, the audit team will review the checklists and notes and write the internal controls audit report. In it, the audit team must state an opinion on the effectiveness of the internal controls.

6.4.3 How to audit financial processes

Financial audits should focus on significant accounts and significant transactions. These are determined by using a top-down, risk-based approach.[6] This means starting at the highest entity and activity levels and doing a risk analysis of the accounting and operations systems. Auditors should try to identify potential risks and assure that responsibilities are identified correctly and that duties are adequately segregated.

---

6. The top-down, risk-based approach is advocated in the new PCAOB audit standard No 5.

The characteristics of significant accounts include the nature of the account, its size and composition, the volume of the activities, its complexity, possible liabilities, and exposure to losses. The auditor should also be aware of changes in the account from prior periods. Significant transactions include cash receipts, cash disbursement, payroll, accounts payable, and disposition of assets.

Examples of entity-level significant accounts are balance sheets, liabilities, and the income statement. Activity-level significant accounts include supply chain management, customer satisfaction information, inventory management, production data, human resources information, information security, and revenue recognition.

A process for evaluating internal controls at the entity and activity levels consists of the following steps:

1. Determine the key processes and significant accounts.
2. Identify key controls in those accounts.
3. Understand the design and operating effectiveness of each control.
4. Understand the supply chain controls and obtain evidence that they operate effectively.
5. Understand the IT infrastructure and controls.

The identification of key controls starts with a review of all controls associated with the significant accounts. Auditors must understand the flow of significant transactions through the accounting processes to the financial statements. Finally, they must determine the key controls that could have a material effect on the major program or financial statements if they were to fail.

Evaluating internal and external service providers starts with an understanding of the operations of the controls that are relevant to the entity's internal control system. Auditors must then obtain evidence that the controls are operating effectively and review the time period covered by the tests of controls, their relation to the date of management's assessment, the scope of the examination and applications covered, the results of tests, and the auditor's opinion on the effectiveness of the controls.

Key controls are tested by running or reviewing transactions to see if they were done correctly. There are generally three types of transactions: recurring financial activities reflected in the accounting records that occur during the normal course of business (sales, cash receipts, payroll, etc.), activities that occur only periodically (taking physical inventory), and estimation based on management's judgments or assumptions (estimating the cost of a new program).

The auditors should randomly pick transactions for different days to see if they were done correctly. Look for triggers. Were the procedures followed? A second method is to generate correct and incorrect items using a "sandbox" and print forms and reports to verify transactions and data.

For some of the key controls, the auditors should do walkthroughs and look for assurance of segregated duties where the person who validates payment of invoices isn't the one who writes the check. The key controls should be identified and tested.

Correct any deficiencies observed during the audit. Experience with process audits will provide insight into value-added auditing that focuses on continual improvement of the management system. Auditors will support the management review of internal controls by:

- Developing corrective action and a remediation plan
- Monitoring the implementation of corrective actions
- Providing an opinion on the effectiveness of the controls

The documentation of audit results must focus on identification of control gaps. It should show the results of the tests for design and operating effectiveness. It should also include the identification and testing of compensating controls as a means of protecting against common fraud activities.

Management should establish a multi-year review cycle for auditing the key internal controls. The schedule should include a review of all assessable units and significant accounts at least every three years.

6.4.4 How to audit quality management systems

A key tool is the process approach defined in ISO 9001's clause 4.1, General requirements. The clause requires identification of the processes needed for the QMS; their sequence and interaction; methods of assuring their effectiveness; provision of necessary resources and information required for their operation; and monitoring, measurement, operation, and improvement of the processes. This should be extended to include financial processes.

In addition to the requirements of clause 4.1, the organization should identify a process owner and the inputs, activities, outputs, objectives, targets, and metrics for each process. A process is a transformation of inputs to outputs, constrained by controls and resources. This is described graphically in figure 6.2.

To identify the steps used to audit a process-based system, an auditor needs to identify the processes of the system and the owner of each process. Then he or she needs to understand the inputs and outputs of each process, determine the

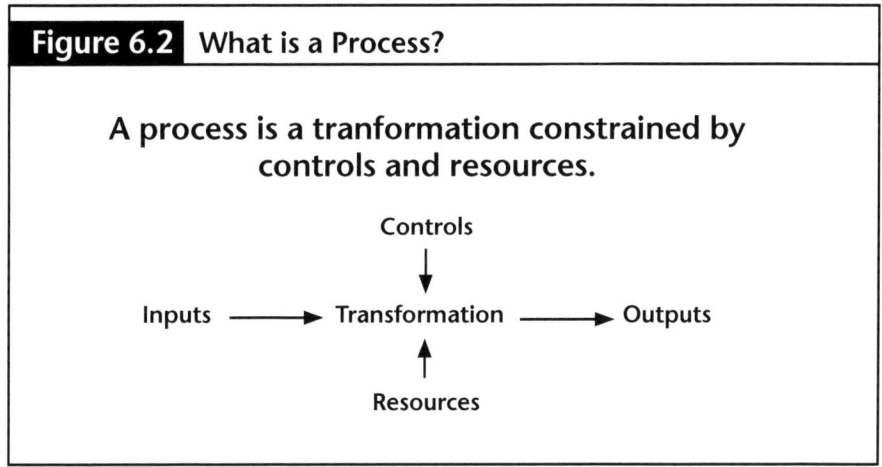

Figure 6.2 What is a Process?

A process is a tranformation constrained by controls and resources.

Controls

Inputs ⟶ Transformation ⟶ Outputs

Resources

resource and control constraints, and understand the activities of each process in terms of the plan-do-check-act (PDCA) improvement cycle.

Three key questions the auditor needs to ask are:

■ Do the processes work together to form a system?
■ How do you define and measure the effectiveness of the QMS?
■ Is the QMS effectively implemented?

There are eight basic processes of any management system. They are:

■ Control of the management system
■ Management involvement
■ Customer focus
■ The improvement process
■ Design and development
■ Supplier management
■ Product and/or service provision
■ Resource management

What is different about auditing a process-based management system? In the past, compliance audits tended to be simple yes/no checklists. They didn't look at the organization's structure in terms of its processes. Processes link elements in various clauses of management standards such as ISO 9001 and ISO 14001. Many processes are cross-functional or involve several departments. Process auditing starts by looking at how processes function. Also, process auditors build their audits around open-ended questions such as, "How do you document your methods and procedures?" PDCA is the tool many organizations use to define their activities.

The following is a description of how an organization can conduct a QMS audit:

1. Develop a business process overview that includes quality and financial processes and a description of the organization's goals and objectives.
2. Conduct a detailed audit of the quality manual and other key documents.
3. Identify the organization's major processes.
4. Look at linkages between processes.
5. Determine whether processes are integrated to form a system.
6. Determine whether the eight basic processes are covered.
7. Develop a three-year audit schedule.
8. Develop checklist questions for each process based on a PDCA description of the processes.
9. Interview process implementers starting with the process owner.
10. Obtain objective evidence including testing of controls used in operations.
11. Identify findings and opportunities for improvement.
12. Document a description of the processes, findings, and opportunities for improvement in an audit report.

Figure 6.3 provides an example of using PDCA to audit the improvement process.

6.4.5 The FDA's Quality System Inspection Technique[7]

The U.S. Food and Drug Administration (FDA) has developed the Quality System Inspection Technique (QSIT) for medical devices. The technique is also useful for the inspection of general QMS because it uses a top-down approach to auditing.

The top-down approach starts with looking for quality problems in the organization's systems. Did they define and document procedures and are those procedures effective? The auditors then look for specific quality problems by sampling records. This is much more effective and less costly than a bottom-up process that starts with the records and works it way up to the system processes.

---

7. The U.S. Food and Drug Administration, "Quality System Inspection Technique (QSIT)," Washington, D.C., August 1999, *www.fda.gov.*

Figure 6.3 | Auditing the Improvement Process

Plan
- Audit top management responsibilities.
- What is the quality policy? How was it transmitted throughout the organization? (clause 5.3)
- What are the measurable objectives? (clause 5.4.1)
  - How are they set?
  - Have objectives been established for the various functions and levels throughout the organization and do they align with the quality policy? (clause 5.3)

Do
- Review the QMS system planning. (clauses 5.4.2, 7.1, and 8.1)
- Is there a method or procedure established for managing the "improvement loop"? (clause 8.5.1)
- Who is responsible for implementation?
- How do they demonstrate the improved effectiveness of the management system?

Check
- Review the following:
  - Internal and external audit results (clause 8.2.2)
  - Data obtained from processes (clause 8.2.3) and products (clause 8.2.4).
  - Analysis of data including:
    - Evaluating where continual improvement of the effectiveness of the QMS can be made (clause 8.4)
    - Did the analysis lead to corrective and preventive actions?
    - Were trends in the data identified and used?

Act
- Review the corrective and preventive actions taken. (clauses 8.5.2 and 8.5.3)
- Review the results of the management reviews. (clause 5.6)
  - What were the management review inputs (clause 5.6.2) and outputs (clause 5.6.3)?
  - What actions were taken?

QSIT focuses on four major processes: management, design controls, production and process controls, and corrective and preventive actions (CAPA). The process approach is an effective way of analyzing each of these processes. QSIT also identifies the following satellite processes: records/documents change control, material control, and facility and equipment controls.

Finally, it identifies four satellite processes specifically for the medical device industry.

Combining the process approach of ISO 9001[8] with the top-down approach of QSIT can be used to develop an effective auditing philosophy.

6.4.6 How to audit environmental management systems

In many ways, auditing an EMS is similar to auditing a QMS. The process approach should be used to structure the audit. All environmental management processes should be identified.

The organization needs to describe the processes that form the EMS, their sequence and interaction, methods of assuring their effectiveness, provision of necessary resources and monitoring, measurement, operation, and improvement of the processes. For each process the process owner needs to be identified as well as the inputs, outputs, suppliers, customer resources, and constraints.

EMS uses many processes similar to those of a QMS. In ISO 14001, tables B.1 and B.2 of appendix B contain the correspondence between ISO 9001 clauses and ISO 14001. These clauses link QMS and EMS and their audits. The main differences between elements of the two standards are the requirements in ISO 14001 to identify environmental aspects and to determine those aspects that have or can have significant effects on the environment. The organization must also determine how legal and other requirements apply to these items.

Aside from these few differences, auditing an EMS is similar to auditing a QMS. Some organizations will conduct quality and environmental audits simultaneously to reduce the resources needed. Doing this also presents an opportunity for organizations to understand each other and learn ways of linking their efforts.

6.4.7 Linking financial, quality, and environmental management audits

A project should be developed to link financial, QMS, and EMS audits. Project oversight is top management's responsibility. Top management consists of the CEO, CFO, vice presidents of quality and environment, and the senior managers that report to them. They participate on a project steering committee, provide advice and recommendations to the project teams, monitor progress and direction

---

8. Paul C. Palmes, *Process-Driven Comprehensive Auditing*, 2nd Ed. (ASQ Quality Press, 2009).

of the project, and act as facilitators between external auditors and the internal audit team.

Audits should be led by senior financial, quality, and environmental managers. They monitor the goals of the internal audit, provide existing documentation for processes in the audit scope, advise on best practices, provide training on project and risk control awareness, and communicate with the external auditors. They also advise management regarding design, scope, and frequency of testing.

Because audits are conducted over extended periods of time, it's necessary to conduct ongoing monitoring and testing. Financial and quality/environmental audits are conducted separately as part of an overall project. However, to be effective, each audit team should have at least one member from other disciplines.

Chapter 2 described the relationship between the COSO guidance and ISO 9001. Figure 6.4 summarizes this relationship and can be used to help auditors link quality management and financial management and define an effective, system of internal control.

The audit team members act as independent assessors of the management testing and assessment process. They test the effectiveness of internal controls to ensure that the processes and controls are operating as designed. As part of the ongoing process, the audit team identifies control gaps, performs follow-up reviews of the gap fixes, assures that the corporate internal controls are well managed, and determines whether they are having a positive effect on the organization.

The project team should periodically conduct a review of the system of internal control. The following questions should be asked:
- Are they having a positive effect on the organization?
- Are they effectively using a top-down, risk-based approach?

The team will monitor the status of existing corrective actions and initiate new ones as issues are identified. The team will also act as coordinator between management and the external auditor regarding scope and test plans of the compliance audits.

Financial management internal audits last longer than quality and environmental management audits because the testing is more extensive and may cover a period of months. That is why there is a need to periodically hold meetings between the audit teams to communicate weaknesses and corrective actions. In addition, regular joint management reviews should be held to communicate these and other issues.

Figure 6.4   Relationships Between ISO 9001, ISO 14001, and COSO

ISO 9001/COSO	Management system	Management responsibility	Resource management	Product realization	Measurement, analysis, and improvement
Internal control environment	■ QMS general requirements (clause 4.1)	■ Management commitment (clause 5.1 ■ Quality policy and objectives (clauses 5.3 and 5.4.1) ■ Internal communication (clause 5.5.3) ■ Resources, roles, responsibilities, and authority (ISO 14001 clause 4.4.1) ■ Emergency preparedness and response (ISO 14001 clause 4.4.7)	■ Provision of resources (clause 6.1) ■ Competence, awareness, and training (clause 6.2.2)	■ Planning product realization (clause 7.1) ■ Operational control (ISO 14001 clause 4.4.6)	■ Planning, measurement, analysis, and improvement (clause 8.1)
Information and communication	■ Control of documents (clause 4.2.3) ■ Control of records (clause 4.2.4)	■ Internal commitment and communication (clauses 5.1 and 5.5.3)	■ Competence, training, and awareness (clause 6.2.2)	■ Determine requirements related to product (clause 7.2.1) ■ Customer communication (clause 7.2.3) ■ Purchasing (clause 7.4)	■ Analysis of data (clause 8.4)
Risk assessment	■ Control of outsourced processes (clause 4.1, last paragraph)	■ Quality objectives (clause 5.4.1) ■ Management review (clause 5.6)	■ Infrastructure (clause 6.3)	■ Customer-related processes (clause 7.2) ■ Purchasing (clause 7.4) ■ Environmental aspects and identification of significant aspects (ISO 14001 clause 4.3.1)	■ Monitoring and measurement (clause 8.2) ■ Data analysis (clause 8.4) ■ Improvement (clause 8.5) ■ Evaluation of compliance (ISO 14001 clause 4.5.2)

ISO 14001 references are shown with an "ISO 14001" in parenthesis and a clause number, other numbers in parenthesis alone are ISO 9001 references.

Figure 6.4	Relationships Between ISO 9001, ISO 14001, and COSO (continued)				
ISO 9001/COSO	Management system	Management responsibility	Resource management	Product realization	Measurement, analysis, and improvement
Monitoring	■ Control of documents (clause 4.2.3) and records (clause 4.2.4)	■ Quality objectives (clause 5.4.1) Management review (clause 5.6)	■ Competence, awareness, and training (clause 6.2.2)	■ Customer-related processes (clause 7.2)	■ Monitoring and measurement (clause 8.2) ■ Analysis of data (clause 8.4) ■ Improvement (clause 8.5)
Control activities	■ Effective processes (clause 4.1c)	■ Management review (clause 5.6 and ISO 14001 clause 4.6)	■ Infrastructure (clause 6.3)	■ Verification of purchased products (clause 7.4.3)	■ Control of nonconforming products (clause 8.3) ■ Improvement (clause 8.5 and ISO 14001 clause 4.5.3) ■ Emergency preparedness and response (ISO 14001 clause 4.4.7)

6.4.8 How to audit information technology systems[9]

Information technology systems are extremely important to all management systems. Each management system may require specific software, but the principles of operation and auditing methodology are the same.

The first step is to understand the IT environment, which includes computer operations and applications and how they link back to the organization. During the preparation process, auditors should inventory the hardware, software, network, and data components, and assess their associated risks. These risks are higher for the parts of the system connected to the Internet.

The risk assessment will depend on the organization's industry sector, size, complexity, and geographic location. Important factors to review are the technologies used, the complexity of the IT environment, the degree of IT centralization, the complexity of business applications, the maintenance operations (including outsourcing), and the stability of the IT environment. Risk tools similar to those used in chapter 3 can be used to ascertain the level of each risk.

An important factor is the level of change that the organization is going through over time. The IT organization should periodically evaluate the risk due to changes in technologies. The chief audit executive (CAE) and the audit team should understand how the IT department's plans would affect risks to the system. At the start of each audit, the CAE and audit team should review the current risk assessment. Audit plans should be flexible and adapt to changes such as new hardware or software and changes in personnel.

If the organization uses tools like CobIT and the ISO 27000 series to structure its IT systems, the auditors should review how they were used. This preparation will give the audit team an understanding of the business processes, the IT environment, and the risks existing in the IT system. This information is then used to develop the audit plan and proceed with the audit. Note that separate audits of the software associated with each management system should be considered by the CAE and the audit team.

Consider reading the Global Technology Audit guide series, which were developed by the Institute for Internal Auditors. There are ten guides in the series, which addresses many aspects of IT operations and auditing.

---

9.   *Developing the IT Auditing Plan* (The Institute of Internal Auditors, 2008).

6.5 IMPLEMENTATION OF LINKED MANAGEMENT SYSTEMS

Linking management systems will help organizations better utilize their core processes, reduce duplication and implementation costs, and allow them to implement other standards more quickly and effectively. A key linking requirement is an effective IT management system.

What should an organization look for in a linked system? First, there should be an improved decision-making process. Budgeting is an operations function based on decisions already made. In reality, it's a management process, not an accounting process. Operations personnel will perform break-even analyses with the help of quality managers. They should understand the profitability of individual products, create the proper product mix, and establish effective budgets for each product.

Second, operations and quality personnel should provide major inputs to strategic planning and management. This includes supply chain management, new product introduction, effective marketing strategies, analysis of research and development, and customer support. Quality management plays key roles in inventory management of raw materials, work in progress, and finished goods.

Finally, quality processes and tools such as Lean Six Sigma will help to improve the bottom line of the organization.

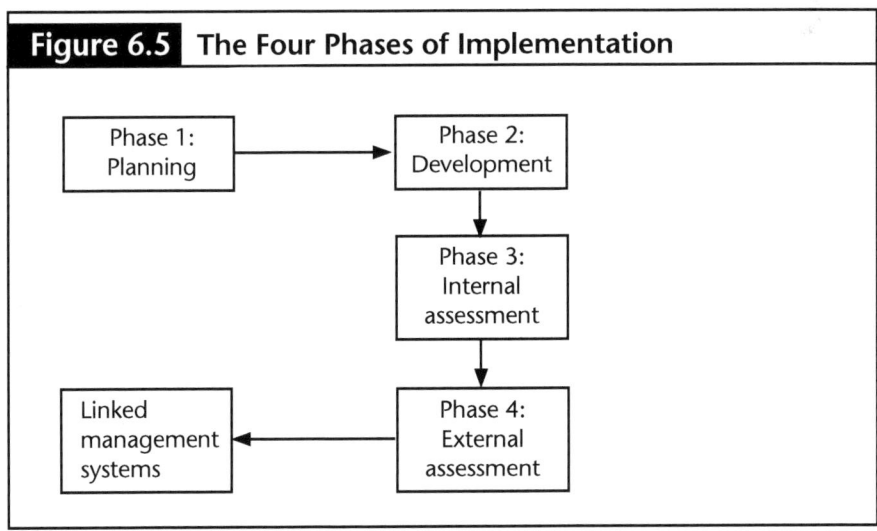

Figure 6.5 | **The Four Phases of Implementation**

The next sections will describe a four-phase system of linking management systems: the planning phase, the development phase, the internal assessment phase, and the external auditing phase. The four phases are shown in figure 6.5.

The planning phase includes developing an understanding of the current business and management practices; training of key members of the staff on the requirements of SOX and ISO standards; identification of gaps in the current business, financial, and quality processes; and guidance in the development of a fully detailed and realistic implementation schedule.

During the development phase, the organization should update the quality manual, standard operating procedures (SOPs), associated work instructions (WIs), and record keeping that satisfy the requirements for the system of internal control. This phase includes training the internal auditors.

The third phase includes planning and conducting complete internal financial, quality, IT, and environmental audits. Corrective actions are accomplished for weaknesses identified during this phase.

The final phase consists of the audits conducted by the external financial, quality, IT, and environmental auditors. Top management should interact with the senior auditors during this phase.

6.5.1 Implementation phase I: planning

Before starting the implementation process, the organization needs to establish a program governance team composed of senior financial, quality, environmental, IT and operations managers, program leaders, and a subteam of implementers. The team should include the leaders who are responsible for the development, evolution, and oversight of the internal controls program. They are responsible for ensuring that the linkage process is performed in a thorough, effective, and timely manner.

Senior leadership must communicate the importance of internal control to the organization and set the tone of the project by communicating the critical nature of linkage to the success of an internal control program. There must be positive, visible actions to build a culture where internal control is valued. Senior leadership must set a tone that includes integrity and ethical values.

The team is responsible for evaluating results, providing recommendations to senior management, and monitoring the development and implementation of corrective action and remediation plans.

A framework must be developed that includes definition of the program scope, activities, and execution; specification of roles and responsibilities; identification of timelines for program execution; and establishment of a senior assessment team. The team should leverage past experience, work on internal control, and integrate with strategic initiatives.

The major responsibilities of the senior assessment team are to determine the overall approach, manage the implementation activities, and determine how the program will be administered. It should leverage past work done on internal control. The team determines the requirements with regard to component units, multiple locations, and cross-unit responsibilities. A top-down, risk-based approach should be used that will focus the organization's resources on the programs that are of greatest risk and accounts that provide the most information to the organization's financial reporting.

A management control plan is the key to the overall approach. It is used to prioritize the evaluation and testing of controls and identify the assessable units that should be reviewed. The plan should also designate the significant accounts, key processes, control objectives, control activities, and risks. Other factors, such as significant reports and material weaknesses, should also be considered when determining the significant accounts to be reviewed.

A material weakness is defined as a deficiency or a combination of deficiencies in internal control over financial reporting, such that there is a reasonable possibility that a material misstatement of the company's annual or interim financial statements won't be prevented or detected. For example, a material weakness occurs when there are a lack of controls in place to ensure reconciliation of intercompany material transfers, such as inventory transfers, allocation of research-and-development costs, and corporate charges.

Another important part of the planning function is to determine the key processes of the organization. Key processes are the primary activities performed within a significant account or assessable unit. Identifying key processes helps to determine and evaluate the internal controls associated with each assessable unit. The key processes should include key controls. The organization should document the key processes using one or more of the following tools:

- Organizational charts
- Flowcharts
- Questionnaires
- Cycle and process memorandums
- Checklists
- Related objectives

The documentation should be current; contain enough detail to describe each process; and show how the processes relate to the major programs, financial re-

Figure 6.6	Example of a Key Process: Budget Execution			
Key process	**Control objective**	**Control activities**	**Risk**	**Risk rating**
Budget execution	Ensure that there is not an over allocation of funds.	■ Individual allocations are reconciled to total allocations prior to distribution. ■ Budget distributions are authorized in writing by an approving official.	Budget allocation (allotment) exceeds apportioned funds	H
	Ensure that the status of funds is monitored periodically.	■ Fund managers report spending against allocations on a monthly basis to the budget officer. ■ The budget officer conducts a quarterly review and analysis meeting to determine the status of funds	Allocated funds are under- or over-obligated.	H
	Ensure that the budget is executed efficiently and effectively.	■ The budget is executed according to a published budget schedule. ■ The budget officer takes control of funds at year end to ensure a fully executed budget.	The budget is not fully executed in a timely manner.	H

porting assertions, potential errors or misstatements, and control objectives. Figure 6.6 is an example of a key process.

The final element of the planning process is to assess the organization's risks of not satisfying the control objectives. This may occur if control activities are not implemented or functioning as intended. Management should assess the risks of misstatement for each key control, document the assessment, and use the results to prepare the testing plan.

An important part of phase one is to run a comprehensive workshop that describes the philosophy, elements, and implementation activities in support of the system of internal control. This includes an understanding of the components of the COSO system of internal control. The workshop should be organized around the major financial and quality processes. Each process is linked to specific elements of the internal controls.

The goals of the workshop are education of the work force and development of a gap analysis of the linked management system with respect to internal control requirements. The workshop looks at processes for maintaining records, assurance of transactions, and methods of protecting company assets. The gap analysis will be extended to follow-up discussions with key personnel. The results are documented in a form that will lead to the creation or updating of the quality manual, SOPs, work instructions, and record keeping in phase two.

The final activity in phase one is to develop and document a plan for the next three phases. The plan defines required resources, tasks, priorities, training, schedules, links to other business processes, and the deliverables of phases two, three, and four. The project team leadership should report its progress regularly to top management and the board of directors.

6.5.2 Implementation phase 2: development

During the development phase, the organization expands its analysis of its financial, quality, environmental, and IT management processes and procedures. The lessons learned from phase one and the analysis are used to revise the organization's procedures and related documentation. This will result in an updated quality manual, process descriptions, and work instructions. It includes the COSO guidance documents and financial processes such as purchase order approval and the preparation of budgets and forecasts. The basis for this activity is the current business management system and the gap analysis from phase one.

The philosophy should be to limit the amount of process documentation required by the standards and documents that support the internal controls. The system should not be so heavily documented that it creates waste and is difficult to manage. Flowcharts should be used extensively. Phase two will also include training of other members of the organization.

The following are the phase two deliverables:

- Revised quality manual, SOPs, records, and work instructions
- A document describing the system of internal control and its relationship to ISO 9001 and ISO 14001
- ISO 9001, ISO 14001, and internal controls training of personnel responsible for the provision of products/services, risk management, and financial activities

6.5.3 Implementation phase 3: internal assessment

Before it starts to link its management systems, an organization must have already completed its individual quality and environmental compliance audits and have passed the external audit of its financial management system. As part of phase three, internal auditors should complete their respective internal audits. ISO 9001 section 8.2.2 provides an overview of how the organization should conduct its internal audits. The results of these audits ensure the effective operation of these management systems.

To start a linked audit, the financial and quality internal auditors will develop a linked audit plan. The following is a sample plan that consists of six activities:

1. Assure the linkages between ISO 9001, ISO 14001, and COSO using figure 6.4.
2. Identify key controls.
3. Evaluate the internal controls at the entity and activity levels.
4. Evaluate internal controls at service providers and suppliers.
5. Test controls.
6. Document the audit results.

The first activity is aimed at ensuring that the internal controls are effective. The linkages will provide substance to the COSO guidance and give auditors an opportunity to review the documentation of each COSO element. At this point, the auditors need to determine whether to proceed with the audit or have the organization correct any problems it identefes.

The second activity starts with the identification of all controls associated with major programs. The team must understand the flow of significant transactions through the accounting processes to the financial statements. It's important that the team understand the IT infrastructure and controls. There must be a subsequent effort to identify the key controls that could have a material effect on major programs or financial statements.

After identifying the key controls, the team must evaluate them at the entity and activity levels. This requires understanding the key processes and identifying the key controls. The design and internal supply chain of each control must then be reviewed and understood. The team must also obtain evidence that the controls are operating effectively.

To evaluate internal controls at service organizations, the team must obtain an understanding of the controls that are relevant to the organization's internal control system and then obtain evidence that the controls are operating effectively by reviewing audit reports, SAS 70[10] reports, or by conducting an on-site audit. SAS 70 is addressed in appendix D.

The testing of key controls is a vital part of these activities. This consists of performing tests for design and operating effectiveness, identifying control gaps, identifying and testing compensating controls, and documenting the test results. The team must evaluate sufficient evidential matter by considering the time period covered by the test of controls and its relation to the date of management's assessment, the scope of the examination, and applications covered.

Finally, the auditors must review the results of tests and provide an opinion on the effectiveness of the controls and the system of internal control. The results of the audit and corrective actions accomplished should be included in a final report.

Management should establish a multi-year review cycle for testing the key internal controls. The testing should include reviewing all of the assessable units and significant accounts at least every three years.

The following are the phase three deliverables:

■ A completed linked internal audit
■ Evaluation of internal controls at supply and service organizations
■ Evaluation of the effectiveness of the system of internal control
■ Results of corrective actions

6.5.4 Implementing phase 4: external auditing

During phase four, separate audits will be conducted of the financial, quality, and environmental management systems. As the organization prepares for the external audit, its leadership team must pay special attention to the set of controls. It will conduct a final review of the management systems using checklists that will be used in the external audits. This will include training on how to deal with the auditors. Role-playing will be used extensively in the training.

The leadership team must be available to interact with the auditors during the audit. The organization should set up a command post to coordinate its responses to audit questions. Experts must be available to advise the leadership team on responses to the audit questions.

The following are the phase four deliverables:

■ A checklist to prepare for the external audit
■ Training on how to interact with auditors
■ Expert support during the audit

---

10.   A detailed description of SAS 70 can be found at *www.SAS70.com*.

6.6 TWO LINKED CASE STUDIES

Appendix B contains two case studies describing the implementation process. The first was provided by Dexter Hansen, quality assurance/information technology (QA/IT) manager of NVE Corp., a small company that manufactures magnetic sensors. The second case study was provided by Tom Carpenter, director of corporate compliance at the Stonhard division of StonCor Group Inc., describing his organization's implementation experiences. StonCor has 2,370 employees at sixteen locations. It manufactures and installs corrosion protection products and polymer flooring and coatings.

6.7 SUMMARY OF LINKED IMPLEMENTATION

This chapter provides the tools to implement a linked management system. It started with a description of the quality and environmental management system support of internal control. This was a summary of the material presented in chapter 2.

The second part of the chapter described the many different types of controls used by the management systems, their associated risks, and the possibility of gaps identified in their application. Controls are key tools used in monitoring the management systems.

The next part discussed internal auditing from an individual system and from the linked approach. Significant accounts and key controls were defined and their importance in the audits pointed out. The quality and environmental audits use process auditing and corrective and preventive actions to great value. These are tools that can also be used in the financial and IT audits.

The final section described a methodology for linking the three management systems. A four-phased approach consisting of planning, development, internal assessment and external audit was described. This included deliverables for each phase.

Chapter 7 will extend the thinking to specific relationships between the management systems and describe methods that quality and environmental managers can use to create linkages to the financial management systems in their organizations. The chapter includes feedback from two questionnaires describing the processes and tools that organizations must develop to create effective management system linkages.

6.8 CHAPTER 6 EXERCISES: TESTING CONTROLS

Select at least one risk from each category in table 6.1 and complete a control management matrix for selected risks using tables 6.2 through 6.5.

Table 6.1	Risk Categories	
Financial management risk	**Customer satisfaction risk**	**Cycle time risk**

• Accounts payable
• Accounts receivable
• Reconciliation
• Financial reporting
• Budget setting
• Business reviews
• Revenue recognition
• Other
	• On-time delivery
	• Product quality
	  o Return rates
	  o Warranty rates
	• Commitment satisfaction rate
	• Accounts payable triggers
	• Poor communication
	• Other
		• Promised lead time vs. actual lead time
		• Rework/repair time
		• Supply chain cycle time
		• Other

Inventory and cash management risk	**Supply chain risk**	**New product/service risk**
• Inventory days of supply • Days sales outstanding • Days payables outstanding • Cash conversion cycle • Other	• Critical supplier management • Order management • Inventory carrying cost • Supply chain finance and planning • Supply chain IT • Procurement department staffing • Other	• New product/service planning • Design and development • Design verification • Design validation • Design changes • Marketing • Production • Distribution • Other

Table 6.2	Control Management Matrix for _____ (Risk Category) _____				
Risk	Risk level (E, H, M, L)	Control(s) (Select from tables C6.3, C6.4 or C6.5 below.)	Type of control (P, D, C)	Tests	Outcomes

Risk levels
E = Extreme
H = High
M = Medium
L = Low

Type of controls
P = Preventive
D = Detective
C = Corrective

Table 6.3	Entity-Level Controls

1. HR policies
2. Code of conduct
3. Communication strategy
4. Accounting policies
5. Management's risk assessment process
6. Organizational structure
7. Training

8. Classes of transactions and disclosure-related assertions
9. Processing of nonroutine transactions
10. Selection/application of accounting policies
11. Initiating, recording, processing, and reconciling account balances

12. Prevention, identification, and detection of fraud
13. Separation of duties
14. Dual signatures on checks
15. Password policies
16. Reconciliation procedures
17. Ethics policies
18. Other

Table 6.4	Activity-Level Controls

1. Cash
2. Inventory
3. Shipping
4. Product realization/ manufacture/service provision

5. Contract management
6. Accounts receivable
7. IT controls
8. Application controls
9. Security controls

10. Record retention
11. Anti-fraud
12. Accounts payable
13. Revenue recognition
14. Incoming materials
15. Other

Table 6.5	Quality Management System Control	
1. Management review (5.6.1) 2. Training records (6.2.2) 3. Contract review: review requirements (7.2.2) 4. Design-and-development inputs (7.3.2) 5. Design-and-development review (7.3.4) 6. Design-and-development verification (7.3.5) 7. Design-and-development validation (7.3.6)	8. Design-and-development changes (7.3.7) 9. Purchasing evaluations (7.4.1) 10. Validation of special processes (7.5.2) 11. Identification of the product (7.5.3) 12. Customer property lost, damaged, or unsuitable (7.5.4) 13. Calibration records (7.6) 14. Audit records (8.2.2) 15. Authorized release of product (8.2.4) 16. Control of nonconforming product (8.3)	17. Corrective action (8.5.2) 18. Preventive action (8.5.3) **Operational controls** 19. The size and age of inventories 20. Critical supply chain measures 21. Shipment of products 22. Information security 23. Record retention 24. Customer satisfaction 25. Production 26. Human resources 27. Revenue recognition 28. Supply of critical components 29. Other

Note: The numbers in parentheses refer to the corresponding clauses in ISO 9001.

Chapter 7

Lessons Learned from Linked Management Systems

7.1 INTRODUCTION

In 2003, the American Society for Quality (ASQ) formed a Sarbanes-Oxley (SOX) team to investigate the linkage between quality management systems (QMS) and environmental management systems (EMS) with financial management systems. Since then, the team has presented six workshops, a webinar, two ASQ conferences, and a case study conference call. Interest has picked up in the quality community, as well as with the Institute of Management Accountants, the Institute of Internal Auditors, the American Institute of Certified Public Accountants, and the Sarbanes-Oxley Institute.

In September 2005, *Quality Progress* magazine published an article[1] describing the relationship between ISO 9001 and ISO 14001 and SOX's basic internal control tool, the Treadway Commission's Committee of Sponsoring Organizations guidance document (COSO)[2]. COSO is used to satisfy the key requirement in section 404 of SOX that requires organizations to have an effective system of internal control. In March 2006, *Quality Progress* published a second standards column[3] describing feedback from eight case studies conducted by the ASQ SOX team. The first case study questionnaire is shown in figure 7.1. In November 2007, a second questionnaire was sent out to six organizations. The second questionnaire is described in section 7.5 and shown in figure 7.2.

---

1. Sandford Liebesman, "Mitigate Sox Risk With ISO 9001 and 14001," *Quality Progress*, September 2005, 91–93.
2. "Internal Control—Integrated Framework, Evaluation Tools," Committee of Sponsoring Organizations of the Treadway Commission, September 1993.
3. Sandford Liebesman, "QMSs and EMSs Support Financial Management Systems," Standards Outlook, *Quality Progress*, March 2006, 83–85.

The goal of this chapter is to provide examples of the methodology that quality managers have used to create linkages to their organizations' financial management systems. This chapter will describe the processes and tools organizations should consider using in an effective linkage process. The first case study questionnaire focused on the interaction between quality management and internal financial auditors (IFAs) in support of five key areas of linkage. The second case study gathered information on direct linkages between management systems through key shared quality procedures.

7.2 THE FIRST CASE STUDY QUESTIONNAIRE

QMSs and EMSs can provide help to satisfy more requirements than just those in section 404. To obtain information on this support, the ASQ SOX team developed a questionnaire that was completed by eight case study organizations, which were:

- Otter Tail Corp., an energy and health care provider and manufacturing conglomerate
- Nordham Group, an aerospace supplier
- Intrado Inc., a provider of 911 services
- StonCor Group, a corrosion protection company
- Communication Test Design Inc., a telecommunication equipment repair company
- International Gaming Technology, a supplier of services and equipment to casinos
- Linear Technology Inc., a manufacturer of high-performance analog integrated circuits
- NVE Corp., a manufacturer of magnetic integrated circuits

The questionnaire consisted of five key areas in which an organization's QMS can also support its financial management system, and, in particular, the internal financial auditors in compliance to SOX. The survey results are summarized in figure 7.1 on page 148.

7.2.1 Supporting business process operations

The participants identified value-adding improvements and reductions in operating costs. They also identified nonvalue-added activities and costs that were eliminated by the organizations. The activities supported financial processes such as bids, settlements, mergers, acquisitions, and revenue recognition. Processes familiar to QMS and EMS managers, such as shipping, receiving, nonconforming product, inventory control, and customer focus were sources of valuable inputs to SOX compliance.

7.2.2 Training IFAs to use quality tools

The quality and human resource departments in the participating organizations provided training to financial personnel in the structure of processes, mapping business processes to the system of internal controls, and measuring and auditing them. Part of the training effort consisted of identifying the steps in the product or service realization process. This helped expand the financial personnel's view of the organizations' operations.

7.2.3 Supporting the risk management process

Quality personnel helped plan the risk management process. This included early identification of risks and identification of operational nonconformities and their corrections. The QMS was a source of early identification of risks and corrective and preventive actions that helped the bottom line. Regular internal audits provided valuable information in early risk identification. The management review was extended to include risk management.

7.2.4 Supporting the auditing process

Quality managers led a focus on process audits and the use of risk management indicators. Key elements of the auditing process are identification of nonconformities, determining root causes, corrective actions (CA), and documentation of CA verifications. Audit results can be used to support testing of internal controls and validation of product and process performance measures. Results strengthened alignment of marketing and sales. Some organizations consolidated the audit reports sent to their boards of directors.

7.2.5 Developing business process measures

Measurable objectives—a key requirement of ISO 9001—were developed and implemented at the participating organizations and used in process and product (or service) improvement. Objectives are an important part of the ISO 9001 improvement process, which also includes the quality policy, audit results, analysis of data, corrective and preventive actions (CAPA), and management review. An effective improvement process can provide evidence of the "tone at the top."

7.2.6 Continued learning from the case study participants

After completion and analysis of the case studies, the SOX team continued its interaction with the eight study participants. The next two sections reflect on the continued lessons learned from participant conference calls, e-mails, and feedback during presentations and SOX conferences.

7.3 LESSONS LEARNED: YEAR ONE

Creating and testing of organizations' financial processes was part of an improvement process. By eliminating redundant items in the financial and quality processes, significant time was freed up, allowing more time for performing value-added activities. This resulted in streamlining financial reporting and review activities.

One organization in the study spent a lot of time analyzing its shipping process. Data from shipping were a direct input into accounts receivables and revenue recognition. Another organization confirmed that outputs from the customer service and order processes were adequate and effective for the needs of its finance department.

There were a number of inputs related to risk management. Risk management is driven through the product realization process and is product focused. Contract review is important because it focuses on financial risk. Nonconformance issues are documented and placed in the corrective action system as an aid to early risk identification.

Every step in the product realization process creates a transaction. The advice from one participant was to make sure to identify critical points in each process. This will result in the creation of additional controls.

Some advice on auditing came from one organization that formerly had audited each of its division's financial controls separately. In the past, the same errors were made in each division. Now the organization audits by process, following the processes from division to division. Other suggestions on auditing were to cross-train quality and financial auditors. IFAs learned operational controls, which resulted in opportunities to improve the bottom line. They also met a major goal: ISO 9001 and SOX tests of controls in one audit.

A final piece of advice was to get a fixed price from the external financial auditor. This will result in the auditor's not expanding the audit, reducing the time spent by the audited organization, and limiting the cost of the audit.

7.4 LESSONS LEARNED: YEAR TWO

In year two, the organizations participating in the survey avoided duplication of effort during their audits. They focused on eliminating duplicate tests and integrated ISO and SOX checklists. They also improved communication by holding combined kickoff and debriefing meetings and efficiently distributed audit findings, corrective actions, and preventive actions.

The organizations had to work with two teams of external auditors: financial SOX auditors and third-party auditors. They created an integrated audit findings database and scheduled combined audit segments and separate segments. One organization developed an ISO-SOX overlap matrix that showed the ISO and COSO requirements side-by-side.

For the SOX portion of the audits, the organizations educated their personnel on the criteria in the audit document used by SOX auditors, PCAOB[4] audit standard No. 5. They cross-trained on ISO and SOX criteria, IT and financial controls, fraud protection, and risk management. Most important, they also worked with process owners to identify the key controls and determine techniques to sample the others. One organization developed an integrated audit program chart that included the objectives, control owner, tests used, results (including deficiencies), and corrective actions for each control item.

Year two results showed improvement in cost of compliance for the case studies with one organization reducing its cost by 60 percent. The key to this large reduction was obtaining a fixed price for its yearly services from third-party auditors.

7.4.1 Feedback from the first case study participants

During the three years of the study, numerous discussions were held with the case study participants and other knowledgeable people about improving the linkages between their management systems. The rest of this section provides the participants' comments in the exact wording as they were received. The comments are valuable indications of areas of difficulty and solutions to problems and should help other implementers develop their linkage processes.

7.4.2 Business process operations

The biggest benefit was that the internal financial auditors learned more about the business operations, the work flow, nonconforming situations, and

---

4. Public Company Accounting Oversight Board

regulatory requirements. Following are individual comments from the participants.

■ *Product/service realization process.* "We identified value added and/or nonvalue-added activities and costs in the finance process and/or product/service realization processes."

■ *Improvement process.* "The entire creation and testing of the financial processes was an improvement process. However, we did not reduce costs or improve the product quality. We did improve the effectiveness of the financial processes and the products of the financial processes."

■ *Shipping process.* "We spent a lot of time analyzing the shipping process because the output of shipping is a direct input into accounts receivables and revenue recognition. We did not identify cost reductions or product improvements, but we did verify the effectiveness of the interrelation between shipping and the financial processes."

■ *Customer-focused process.* "We spent significant time understanding the interrelationships between customer service, order processing, and the financial processes. It's not clear that we improved customer satisfaction, but we did confirm that the outputs from customer service and order processing are adequate and effective for the needs of the finance department."

■ *General business processes.* "While documenting our financial processes, we found several areas with redundant and/or unnecessary reports or steps. By eliminating them, significant amounts of time were freed up for several manufacturing/purchasing supervisors, allowing more time for performing value-added activities." "We had already developed and implemented a very robust process improvement program as part of our ISO 9001 enterprise resource planning (ERP) system. This program was utilized extensively to streamline our financial reporting and review activities when putting together our SOX compliance plan." "A task group had already been in place for several years for the purpose of tracking and improving shipping costs, so little more needed to be added during the SOX abatement activities."

7.4.3 Training process

■ *Process auditing.* "The IFAs learned process auditing, which included identification of internal controls in addition to the financial controls. Every step in the product realization process created a transaction that was an opportunity to improve our bottom line."

■ *Training.* "There was a great deal of reluctance to training anyone other than the president, controller, and CFO. So the controller was caught off guard when

I proposed a simple SOX Internet course with an e-mail quiz certification in the training folders as a record. The auditor said that the Internet training was acceptable. As a result, we're still way ahead of where the consultant and our auditor thought we would be. Internet training is valuable because it can be done anytime and can be used for many separate activities. The quiz/certification provides evidence of the training."

- *Enterprise resource planning (ERP).* "We had a very robust training program already in place as part of our ISO 9001 ERP activities. This program was expanded to include formalized training of the financial employees as the SOX initiative progressed."

7.4.4 Risk management process

- *Nonconformances.* "Nonconformance issues are documented and placed in our corrective action system. Issues are put in at the appropriate responsibility level."

- *Risk management.* "Risk management is required by our customers." "Risk management is driven through the product realization process and is product focused. Changes to the realization process could create additional risks." "Risk management is important with respect to contract review, which translates to financial risk. In other words, there is a need to complete the work on time without additional costs to our business. Also, it is necessary to capture any product changes, get paid for them or learn not to repeat them if they are our fault." "The changes were aimed at making sure we meet the budget/cost projections of our design."

- *ISO 9001 processes.* "Corrective and preventive actions, as well as management review, were already part of our ISO 9001 QMS. The financial aspects associated with SOX were rolled into these existing programs to streamline the assimilation of these tools into the finance areas."

7.4.5 Auditing process

- *Process audits.* "We are learning to conduct process audits and to make sure we considered processes that have critical points." "Our IFAs audited each of our divisions' financial controls. In the past we made the same errors in each division. Now that they are auditing by process and following the process from division to division we can see that the processes are working throughout all divisions simultaneously." "Our organization used both process and compliance audits."

■ *Auditor training.* "The existing group of nine ISO 9001 internal auditors and two new auditors from the finance area were trained in the various SOX requirements. They are now responsible for auditing the company's SOX compliance."

7.4.6 Business process measures

■ *Need to improve.* "Most of our measures are financial and the IFAs understand those measures, but the management review process is something new for them. Our divisions don't do this well (nonvalue-added), so the IFA aren't really getting much value from this effort. This is an area that our company needs to improve."

■ *Integrating processes.* "Each of the components listed in this category had already been integrated into our existing ISO 9001 ERP several years ago. They were expanded to include additional metrics specifically associated with the SOX compliance program."

7.4.7 General comments

■ *ISO 9001 and SOX requirements.* "I think that there would only be a marginal improvement for a company already running a good ISO 9001 system. The value for ISO 9001-certified companies is that they have pretty well have done most of these cost reductions or value-added activities and already have a number of systems in place that meet the SOX requirements."

■ *Tone at the top.* "While I had originally done the ALLTEL survey[5], it was done again in the last fiscal year. Because I have it on the Internet and can dump the data to a data file that drops into Excel, it will take me all of an hour to cut, paste, and summarize." "The only folks I'm collecting data on are the CEO, CFO, controller, and the president's staff. That's the 'tone' evidence and needs to be done annually."

■ *Questionnaire activities.* "We performed nearly all of the five activities described in the first questionnaire as part of SOX compliance and ISO audits, process improvement teams, and ongoing continual improvement efforts. We have not yet implemented a balanced scorecard, although our strategic plan calls for a scorecard of sorts (performance metrics around key areas)."

■ *Integrating ISO and SOX audits.* "We're attempting to integrate our ISO and SOX audits to be more efficient. We'd like to incorporate ISO 9001/quality-related

---

5. *ALLTELL Control and Risk Self-Assessment Processes* (The Institute of Internal Auditors, 2002).

audit questions into our SOX audit programs so that we can accomplish both sets of objectives at once."

■ *Baldrige Criteria self-assessment.* "We're planning to do a Malcolm Baldrige self-assessment later in the year to prepare for an application for our state's quality award. This effort will undoubtedly affect our SOX compliance efforts, as well as our ISO compliance program."

■ *Audit structure.* "Because our customer's financial results were driving the audits, they were structured more toward operations and security (physical and IT) process controls than the financial controls. They weren't much different than full-blown ISO audits. For the SOX audits we had the processes, process flows, procedures, and records thoroughly reviewed to determine the depth of the company's controls. The customer had input to agree or disagree with our controls. The end result was an opinion from the audit house in a formal audit report. We had zero problems and one or two opportunities for improvement."

7.5 THE SECOND CASE STUDY QUESTIONNAIRE

The case study questionnaire on linked management systems is provided in figure 7.2. It's recommended that organizations use it to determine progress during the first few years of linking their management systems.

Six manufacturing organizations provided responses to the second case study questionnaire. These were NVE Corp., Linear Technology, Nordham Group, StonCor Group, 3M Corp., and the Woodridge Group. The first four companies participated in the first case study; 3M is a diversified global technology company and Woodbridge Group is a private company that makes molded foam seating for automobiles.

The six organizations varied in size from small (50 employees and $14.5 million in annual revenue) to very large (70,000 employees and $26 billion in annual revenue). Their levels of management systems linkage varied from complete linkage to partial or informal linkages. The largest organization had the lowest level of management system linkage, illustrating that it's almost always more difficult to link large organizations than small ones.

■ *ISO 9001 processes.* All six organizations in the survey were registered to ISO 9001:2008; five use the ISO 9001 document control procedure, and four use the ISO 9001 records control procedures. The largest organization has separate document control and records control procedures for each of its divisions. The smallest organization has a separate record control system for finance.

- *ISO 9000 improvement processes.* Five organizations use the ISO 9001:2008 preventive action, corrective action, and internal audit procedures for all management systems. The largest organization has separate procedures for each division. Four use a combined management review process, but the smallest and largest have separate management reviews for quality and finance.

- *Risk management.* All of the organizations in the survey have risk management processes. The largest organization is the only one that doesn't have risk appetite and risk tolerance definitions; the smallest one sets risk limits and goals as its definition of risk appetite. The risk management tools most often cited were the risk level matrix, the risk control matrix, FMEA, and management review. Three organizations either used or were implementing enterprise risk management procedures.

- *Key control.* The number of key controls varied from nineteen for the smallest organization to 186 for the largest. Examples of these controls are accounts receivable, accounts payable, payroll, inventory, internal auditing, corrective and preventive actions, and IT controls. The organizations track inventory variances of raw materials and finished goods.

- *IT controls.* All six organizations had a formal system of IT controls. These included access control, records, transactions, journal entries, document control, and internal IT audits. Two organizations use CobIT as a basis for their IT controls.

- *SOX compliance.* Four organizations were SOX compliant, but the other two were private companies and therefore weren't required to comply with SOX. The SOX compliance effort in two organizations was led by the director of corporate compliance and the quality corporate auditor. The CFO was the leader in the other two organizations. The SOX audit team varied in makeup and was generally led by the quality organization.

- *Cost reduction.* The cost of SOX compliance went down every year, with the two smallest organizations cutting their costs by 50 percent after the third year. The cost of compliance in the third year for the two smallest organizations was $22,000 and $60,000, respectively. The other organizations declined to provide cost information.

- *Key changes made during years two and three.* The following contributed to improvements during these years in the four public companies:
  - Better control of computer access
  - Tighter controls and more audit activity
  - Effectiveness increased because of training and improved process definitions

- Internal auditors improved their understanding of process requirements
- Accounts receivable and revenue recognition were combined into one process
- Processes were better defined
- Improved understanding of competence, awareness, and training

■ *Lessons learned.* There are a number of lessons to be learned from these results. The management systems in the two smallest organizations had the greatest level of linkage, resulting in improved resource utilization. The amount of linkage decreased as the size of the organization increased. Organizations should consider using QMS procedures for document control, control of records, corrective action, preventive action, and internal audits. There should be an organizationwide risk control management system so that risks are handled consistently. Quality and IT controls should be included in the system of internal control. Finally, the quality organization should play a major role in the SOX compliance process.

7.6 A LINKED MANAGEMENT SYSTEMS STORY

This narrative was provided by one of the participants in the two questionnaires. The organization is a mid-sized global company with eight locations around the world and annual revenues of about $500 million. The following paragraphs contain her experiences in her own words.

Our corrective action system became overloaded with corrections made without permanent fixes. No one was trying to do anything to improve the situation, and every year the process was repeated with the same results. In addition, it became clear that the quality organization needed to learn the language of financial management.

Things started to change when a new internal financial audit staff was brought in. Also, our audit committee was expanded to include independent members. The quality and financial auditors met and decided to integrate the audits and include SOX/COSO audits. Most important, activities were consolidated and duplicated costs were reduced.

Quality management personnel trained the IFAs on ISO 9001:2008 and financial management personnel trained the quality auditors on internal controls. Quality was responsible for creating a process audit system and the IFAs showed quality auditors the value of increasing audit samples.

When planning how to integrate audits, the two audit organizations determined how they were the same. Functionally, they both focused on good business practices. They used formal audit schedules, trained auditors, and corrective and preventive ac-

tion processes. They also had combined methods of identifying risks to the company. The major differences were the customers of each audit. Quality audits were provided to support compliance to ISO 9001:2008 and identify areas of improvement for operations managers. The customers of the financial audits were top management, the board of directors, and the external auditors.

The two organizations developed methods of sharing the auditing process. They combined checklists, developed methods of exchanging information, and traded sampling results. As for the results, they shared audit information and combined requirements with the findings, but published separate audit reports.

The quality and financial auditors identified four types of data to exchange. For credit memos, the financial auditors reviewed the authorizations and the quality auditors looked at corrective action opportunities. Concerns for design projects were risks and cost for financial auditors and risks and authorizations for quality. Scrap was reviewed for the correct amount by financial auditors and the disposition by quality auditors. Finally, for purchase orders financial auditors reviewed authorizations while quality auditors assured that quality system requirements were included.

Two value-added improvements from this approach were the use of lean events to identify broken processes and improve SAP[6] functioning. The improved supplier management process reduced supply costs and eliminated obsolete inventory transfers, audited supplier activities, and determined why certain suppliers were ineffective. Finally, the two audit teams reported to the audit committee on the combined audits.

ISO 9001 clauses were paired with COSO guidance and financial checklists were developed to audit COSO. Training was provided on measuring and auditing internal controls. This included how to link findings to internal control, assuring compliance of exports to requirements, and assurance of data security. Both sets of auditors were trained in process audits. This enabled the effective auditing of processes across divisions.

It was evident that early identification of risks was very important. This meant identification of risks through effective planning, strong program management, reviewing the use of resources, and assuring that timelines were meaningful. Three particular quality processes were particularly important: preventive action, corrective action, and management review. Effective preventive and corrective actions depended on analysis of data and identification of repetitive findings. The management reviews combined audit results with the analysis of financial effects to the bottom line.

---

6. SAP is a provider of business management software solutions. In this case, SAP refers to the software provided to the organization.

Process audits were used to improve companywide processes, identify best practices, and clarify risks associated with each process. Internal controls were tested and the resulting analysis of the data using the SAP system led to an integration of processes and the combination of some audits. Reporting of material nonfinancial information as part of the SOX results improved process effectiveness, helped identify the right people for certain jobs, and clarified customer and regulatory requirements. Finally, sending consolidated audit reports to the board improved visibility of the quality organization and led to better understanding of the financial results of noncompliance.

Using the audit results and comparing actual costs to quotes led to product and service improvements. Customer satisfaction measures obtained from surveys were used to modify strategic planning. SAP design and development resulted in improved controls within the company and allayed security concerns. These results were reported at management review meetings, which support the old adage: "What gets measured gets fixed."

What does the future hold? The greater use of SAP controls will provide better security through improved control of access to data. Better control of exported products will result from the newly linked documentation and training. Security will be improved by a clearer identification of the end user. And applying the COSO guidance will lead to better management of risk.

The first two joint audits seemed awkward, but eventually the organizations gained confidence. We learned which group took the lead in individual audits and we expanded the scope of our audits. We improved our approach to audit sampling and found ways of combining COSO and ISO requirements. Finally, top management learned the value of quality and gained an appreciation of processes and process auditing.

7.7 OTHER SOURCES OF INFORMATION

The International Organization for Standardization (ISO) recently published a book describing guidance on how to integrate requirements of multiple ISO and non-ISO management system standards.[7] It describes examples from case studies submitted by fifteen organizations that link ISO 9001, ISO 14001, ISO/TS 16949, OHSAS 18001, and other standards. Unfortunately, there is only one brief mention of financial management in any of the case studies.

One example cited in the book is GKN Driveline, a European automotive organization that linked its compliance to ISO 9001, ISO/TS 16949, ISO 13485,

---

7. *The Integrated Use of Management Systems* (International Organization for Standardization, 2008).

ISO 14001, and OHSAS 18001. The company developed common procedures for document control, combined internal audits, combined management reviews, and combined control of information flow in its linkage effort.

A second example in the book is provided by Ferrovial, a European construction firm that linked its quality, environmental, and risk prevention systems. The result of Ferrovial's effort is a system that is less complicated and better understood by everyone in the organization and a consistent combined management system.

The real value of the book is identification of linkage principles that are used in many different environments. The examples validate these principles and provide useful compliance ideas for readers of this book. Two other references on linked management systems are "Management System Integration: Can It Be Done?" (Quality Progress)[8] and *Integrated Management Systems Manual* (Ditech Networks, 2006).[9]

7.8 A FINAL WORD

Linking quality and financial management systems and their associated audits is an opportunity for quality professionals to provide value directly to top management and their organizations' board of directors. It's also an opportunity for quality and financial professionals to learn about each other's activities and language. Finally, it's an opportunity for an organization to reduce the high cost of complying with SOX.

8. Mary McDonald, Terry A. Mors, and Ann Phillips, "Management System Integration: Can It Be Done?" *Quality Progress*, October 2003, 67–74.
9. Ditech Networks, "Integrated Management Systems Manual."

7.9 EXERCISES

7.9.1 Exercise 7.1: Using the first case study questionnaire

The elements in the first case study questionnaire are areas where QMS/EMS practitioners can work with their financial counterparts.

Identify the statements in figure 7.1 that you agree with. Put a checkmark in the left-hand column. The statements that are not checked should be investigated for possible implementation.

7.9.2 Exercise 7.2: Using the second case study questionnaire

I recommend that organizations use figure 7.2 to determine their progress during the first few years of linking their management systems.

Figure 7.1	Results of First Case Study Questionnaire
No. of respondents that agreed with statement	**Business process operations**
	■ Financial operations and controls
3	• Identified nonvalue-added activities and costs in the product/service realization process
6	• Identified value-added improvements and reduced cost in operations
3	• Used the improvement process to reduce costs and improve product/service quality
2	• Used the supplier management process to reduce supply costs and improve product/service quality
1	• Used the shipping process to reduce transportation costs and improve product/service quality. (Please include products or services shipped electronically)
2	• Used the customer focus process to improve customer satisfaction
5	• Supported other financial process (e.g., requests for quotes, bids, settlements, mergers and acquisitions, revenue recognition)
	■ Used the training processes to train internal financial auditors (IFAs) in the following:
5	• Business process attributes
6	• Mapping business processes to COSO
6	• Measuring and auditing internal controls
6	• Process auditing
	■ Supported the risk management process
7	• Planning
5	• Early identification of risks
6	• Nonconformances
5	o Nonconformances managed at various management levels depending on risk levels
5	• Preventive action
7	• Corrective action
5	• Management review

Figure 7.1	Results of First Case Study Questionnaire (cont.)
No. of respondents that agreed with statement	Business process operations
	■ Supported the auditing process
	• Audit planning
7	o Used process audits, not compliance audits
5	o Used risk management indicators
	• Audit results
6	o Supported testing of internal controls
4	o Supported validation of process and product performance measures
2	✓ Confirmation of operational expenses
4	✓ Operations alignment with marketing and sales
4	✓ Traceability of customer requirements from contract review to customer delivery
4	o Reporting of material nonfinancial information
4	• Collaborated with financial auditors on consolidated audit reports to the board of directors' audit committee
	■ Developed the following business process measures:
4	• Documented results of management review meetings
5	• Customer satisfaction measures
5	• Measurable objectives used in product/service improvement
1	• Balanced scorecard. (Please indicate measures used in the scorecard)
4	• Supported the IT organization in development of software quality measures
4	• Supported IT development of improved (expanded) controls within the company

Figure 7.2	Second Case Study Questionnaire: Linked Management Systems
1. Organization information	
a. Organization name	
b. Headquarters location	
c. Number of employees	
d. Number of locations	
e. Annual revenue	
f. Is your organization listed on a U.S. stock and/or bond exchange?	
i. If yes, which one(s)?	
ii. If no, what is the status of your organization (privately held, nonprofit)?	
g. What is your organization's capitalization?	
2. SOX questionnaire contact information	
a. Name	
b. Position/title	
c. Phone number	
d. Fax number	
3. Please indicate your organization's formal management system.	
a. Does your organization have a quality management system (QMS)?	
i. Is your organization registered to ISO 9001:2008?	
ii. Is your organization registered to a sector-specific standard (TL 9000, AS9001, ISO/TS 16949, QS-9000, etc.)? Which ones?	
iii. Is your organization using the Baldrige Criteria?	
b. Do you have a Six sigma program?	
c. Does your organization have an environmental management system (EMS)? If yes, is your organization registered to ISO 14001:2004?	
d. Does your organization have an occupational health and safety management system (OHSMS/OHSAS)?	
e. Are your management systems integrated or linked? If yes, which ones?	

Figure 7.2	Second Case Study Questionnaire: Linked Management Systems (cont.)
4. Sharing of procedures between management systems.	
a. Does your organization use the QMS document control procedure in other management systems? If yes, which management system(s)?	
i. If no, what document control procedures do you use for FMS?	
b. Does your organization use the QMS control records procedure in its other management systems? If yes, which ones?	
i. If no, what control of procedures do you use for the FMS?	
c. Does your organization use the QMS corrective action procedure in its other management patterns? If yes, which ones?	
i. If no, what corrective action procedures are used in the FMS?	
d. Does your organization use the QMS preventive action procedure in its other management systems? If yes, which ones?	
i. If no, what preventive action procedure(s) are used for the FMS?	
e. Does your organization use the QMS internal audit procedure in its other management systems? If yes, which ones?	
i. If no, what internal audit procedure(s) are used for the FMS?	
f. Does your organization use the QMS internal audit procedure in your other management systems? If yes, which management system(s)?	
g. Does your organization do joint or combined audits? If yes, which management systems are covered?	
h. Does your organization use joint management reviews? If yes, which management systems are included in the review (QMS, EMS, FMS, OHSMS/OHSAS)?	

Figure 7.2 Second Case Study Questionnaire: Linked Management Systems (cont.)	
5. Management of risk	
a. Does your organization have procedures for managing risk? If yes, does it include the following?	
i. A definition of risk appetite and risk tolerance.	
ii. What risk management tools do you use? (i.e., risk level matrix, ORCA, FMEA, risk control matrix, etc.)	
iii. Does your organization use an enterprise risk management procedures (COSO: Enterprise Management Integrated Framework)?	
6. Controls	
a. How many key controls does your organization have? Please provide a description of five key controls.	
b. Are product and process controls used to support the key financial controls? If yes, please provide an example.	
c. Is the quality records process used to store results of key controls?	
7. Information technology	
a. Does your organization use a formal system of controls to assure the accuracy of your IT system? If yes, please provide an example of a control.	
b. Is CobIT used as a basis for IT controls?	

Figure 7.2	Second Case Study Questionnaire: Linked Management Systems (cont.)
8. Your organization's SOX compliance during year one	
a. Is your organization SOX-compliant as attested to by an external auditor? If no, when is your organization planning to become compliant?	
b. Your organization's SOX compliance effort.	
i. Who was the SOX champion? (Position, not the name of the person)	
ii. Who led the SOX team? (Position, not the name of the person)	
iii. What units provided members to the SOX team?	
c. What was the greatest difficulty your organization had at the start?	
d. Approximately what was the total cost of compliance during year one? During year two? During year three?	
9. What were key changes made during the year two compliance efforts?	
a. What factors led to differences from year one?	
10. What were key changes made during the year three compliance efforts?	
a. What factors led to differences from year two?	
11. General questions	
a. If your organization's management systems have not been integrated, how is synergy created between them?	
b. Did your organization use a consultant to help integrate or develop synergy between your management systems? If yes, please provide an overview of how this was done.	

Chapter 8

A Foundation for Linking Management Systems

8.1 INTRODUCTION

This book has described how organizations can link their quality, environmental, information technology (IT), and financial management systems and identified the benefits of these systems working together. Linked systems can be used to support compliance to the requirements of the Sarbanes-Oxley Act (SOX).

This chapter begins with a summary of the first seven chapters to emphasize the key points discussed earlier in this book. The second part of the chapter describes an eight-part foundation that organizations should consider as they start the development of their management systems linking program.

8.2 SUMMARY OF THE FIRST SEVEN CHAPTERS

By identifying ways of improving the dialogue between financial, quality, IT, and environmental management systems, personnel in these systems will better understand what their peers in other departments do. Chapter 1 provided quality and environmental managers with an introduction to the language of finance and the effect of operations on the bottom line, while financial managers were shown how quality and environmental managers could help improve financial results. In the long run there will be cost savings, continual improvement of processes and products, and a greater understanding of each other's work and responsibilities.

The description of quality management was based on ISO 9001, including the standard's definition of quality manual, an explanation of the five main clauses of the standard, and a look at the documentation structure. Also included were discussions of Lean Six Sigma (LSS), IT, and environmental management systems (EMS). The review of financial management included investment management, statements of cash flow, the profit and loss statement, the balance sheet, the general ledger, and a system of internal control.

Chapter 1 emphasized the value of **connecting management systems**[1], which includes added resources, reduction in the cost of compliance, and **improved corporate governance**. This chapter contained brief descriptions of the process approach and continual improvement. The last part of the chapter discussed SOX compliance and served as an introduction to chapter 2.

The SOX requirements were introduced in chapter 2, which started with a discussion of specific elements of SOX. It then showed how ISO 9001 and ISO 14001 support compliance to SOX section 404, the requirement for an effective system of internal control. These standards support the **linking of operations to SOX compliance**. This was done by comparing these standards to the five Treadway Commission's Committee of Sponsoring Organizations (COSO) elements. Chapter 2 indicated specific clauses in the standards that provide the areas of support and concluded that the support of Quality Management Systems (QMS) and EMS will help top management and the board of directors identify business risks, control them, and prevent major surprises. It was pointed out that the ISO 9001 requirements for six documented procedures results in these procedures being available for use in the financial management and other management systems.

A risk management methodology was defined in chapter 3, which includes key tools for managing and mitigating risks. The risk management process consists of defining the organization's objectives, specifying the risk categories, identifying risks to the objectives, and developing methods for managing them. The four major types of risks: strategic risk, organizational risk, compliance risk, and operational risk were discussed. Operational risk includes ineffective management system risk, customer satisfaction risk, supply chain risk, revenue recognition risk, information security risk, logistics risk, and risks from natural disasters. The last part of the chapter covered **risk analysis methodology**.

Chapter 4 discussed the **role of IT**. An effective IT system is a necessity in the operation of any business. Multiple software applications are needed to run an organization. These include financials, sales, customer service and support, inventory management, enterprise resource planning (ERP), marketing, human resources, and others. IT is also very important for SOX compliance.

Chapter 4 described the structure of a general-purpose computer as having five major parts: the control system, memory storage devices, input and output

---

1. Items in **bold** in section 8.2 provide background for the effective linking of management systems described in section 8.3. I recommend that the reader re-visit the chapters referenced for a better understanding of the eight-part foundation described in section 8.3.

devices, software, and computer networking systems. Chapter 4 also looked at the effect IT has on SOX, specific internal controls, and information security. It was suggested that the ISO 27000 series of standards and the CobIT framework are two excellent tools for assuring the effective management of information security.

Chapter 5 described how LSS links to financial management, ISO 9001, ISO 14001, and IT. The projects implemented as part of the LSS program generate value to the customer and to the organization. However, they cannot operate in a vacuum. They require the support of effective financial, quality, environmental, and other management systems. LSS includes tools that can be used to provide **continual improvement as defined in ISO 9001**.

The discussion of lean focused on a discussion of various types of waste and tools used to understand the wastes and reduce them. The discussion of Six Sigma included tools such as define, measure, analyze, improve, and control (DMAIC) and design for Six Sigma (DFSS). Chapter 5 also included a description of the key personnel that are required to make LSS effective. Examples were given of linking LSS to financial management, quality and environmental management, and IT.

Chapter 6 described the structure of a linked management system and indicated what management must do to assure its effectiveness. Important parts of such a system are the controls used to determine its effectiveness. It also discussed the key controls and their importance in auditing organizations.

A linked or integrated internal auditing system is essential for understanding the status of the overall management system. Chapter 6 discussed separate audits of financial management, quality management and environmental management systems, and audits of the linked management system. Chapter 6 also discussed separate audits of information technology systems.

The remainder of chapter 6 described a methodology for implementing a linked management system. The implementation process consists of four phases: planning, development, internal assessment, and external auditing. Internal assessment is a key tool for **implementing continual improvement**. The description included deliverables for each phase.

Chapter 7 described a set of case studies of organizations that linked their management systems to comply with SOX section 404. The ASQ SOX team used two questionnaires to understand how a set of sample organizations accomplished their linking activities. The first questionnaire was answered by eight organizations and covered five categories:

- Financial operations and controls
- Training internal financial auditors to do process auditing
- Supporting the risk management process
- Linking their auditing process
- Developing business process measures

The results illustrated how quality management systems can support the financial management system and in particular financial auditors.

The second case study questionnaire was completed by six manufacturing organizations. The smallest organizations had the greatest amount of linkage between their management systems. Topics covered included:

- ISO 9001 processes
- Risk management
- Key controls
- SOX compliance
- Sharing of procedures between management systems
- Information technology

The following were lessons learned:

- All management systems should consider using the QMS procedures for document control, control of records, corrective action, preventive action, and internal audits.
- A corporatewide risk-control management system is needed so that risk is handled consistently throughout the organization.
- Quality and IT controls should be included in the system of internal control.
- The quality organization should play a major role in the SOX compliance process.

Chapter 7 included a linked management system story that illustrated how an organization improved communication between quality and financial auditors. This resulted in better communication of information, integrated audits, use of lean events to identify broken processes, and the improvement of the data management system. Checklists should be developed based on pairing ISO 9001 clauses with COSO guidance. Key results affecting the **bottom line included a more effective risk management process**, use of process audits throughout the organization, and use of new customer satisfaction measures to modify strategic planning.

Finally, chapter 7 included examples of case studies from an ISO book[2] that provides guidance on how to integrate requirements of multiple ISO and non-ISO management system standards. The case studies describe a number benefits, including eliminating redundancies, establishing consistency, reducing bureaucracy, optimizing processes and resources, reducing maintenance, consolidation of assessments, improving decision making, use of the process approach, PDCA modeling, and process-based assessments.

8.3 LINKING MANAGEMENT SYSTEMS: A FOUNDATION[3]

After studying the ISO 9001 support of financial management, the ASQ SOX team observed opportunities for linking all management systems within an organization. The feedback we received from organizations was that independent management systems often result in duplication of effort, unnecessary complexity, and higher cost of operations because of the silo effect from management systems not communicating with each other.

Early in the SOX team's effort, it became clear that the biggest problem facing organizations in their compliance efforts was the cost of compliance. Linking management systems provides a number of positive results. First, the QMS and EMS add compliance resources. Second, joint internal audits reduce auditing time and cost and eliminate redundancy during individual audits. Separate audits often result in redundant auditor questions. Third, linked audits improve identification of real-time disclosures. Finally, the support that quality and environmental management gives to financial management can improve revenue recognition, purchasing, and inventory management.

Also during these early efforts the team developed a workshop, which was presented at seven different venues. It became evident that there were major actions that should be performed as part of the linking process. The SOX team proceeded to define of a series of eight actions that constitute a foundation for effective linking of management systems.

---

2. *The Integrated Use of Management Systems* (International Organization for Standardization, 2008).
3. Sandford Liebesman, "Where SOX and Your QMS Converge," *Quality Digest*, September 2007.

8.3.1 The effective linking of management systems

The eight actions necessary to link management systems are shown in figure 8.1.

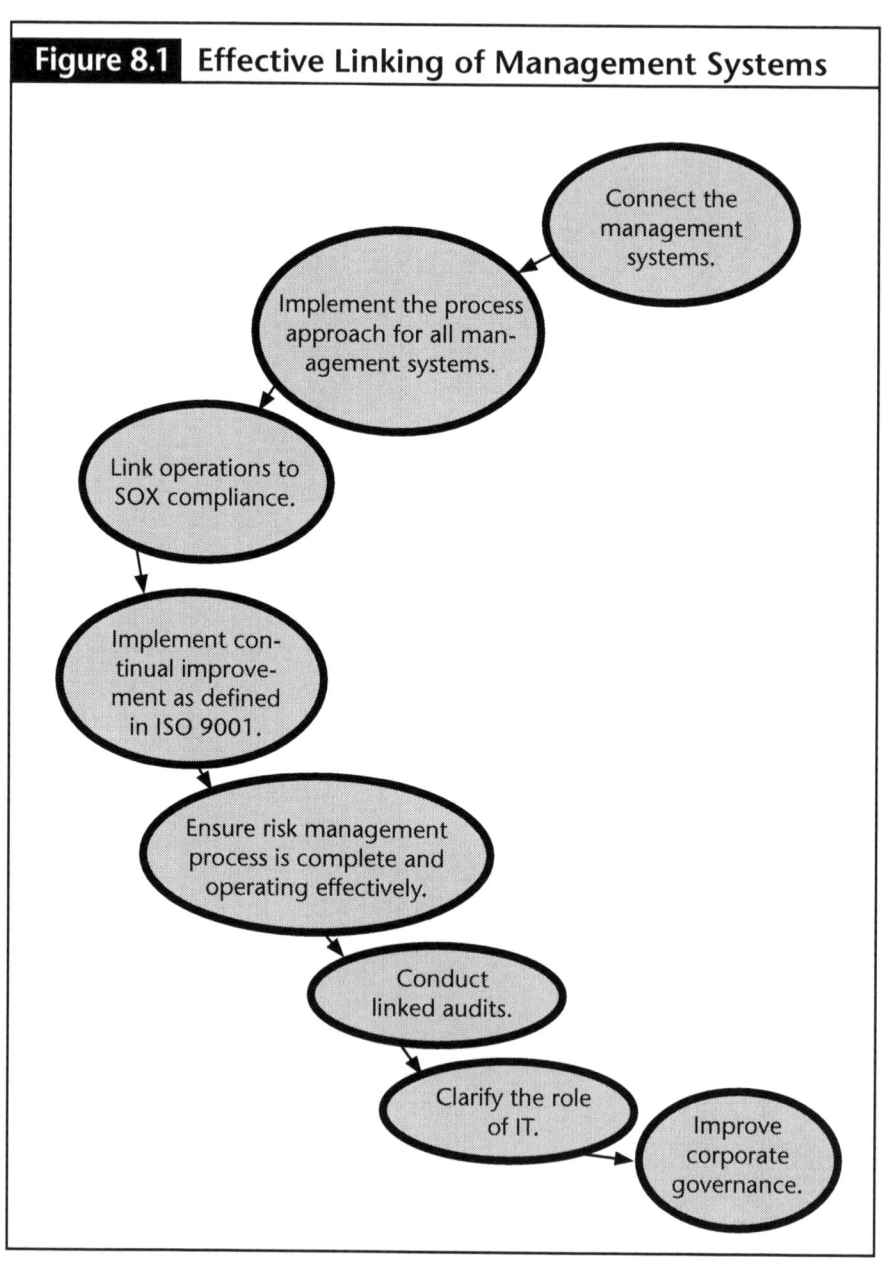

Figure 8.1 Effective Linking of Management Systems

The first action[4] is to connect the management systems by using common processes to reduce duplicated efforts. ISO 9001 provides a basic structure for connecting management systems. The standard requires six documented procedures that can be used by the other management systems are:

■ *Document control* (clause 4.2.3) requires approval, updating, identification of changes and current revision status, availability at point of use, legibility and readability, controlled distribution, and preventing the use of obsolete documents.

■ *Control of records* (clause 4.2.4) says that records must be legible, identifiable, and retrievable. Controls are needed for identification, storage, protection, retrieval, retention time, and disposition.

■ *Corrective action* (clause 8.5.2) requires reviewing nonconformities (including customer complaints), determining causes of nonconformities, evaluating the need for action, determining, implementing, and recording the actions, and reviewing the corrective actions taken.

■ *Preventive action* (clause 8.5.3) requires determining potential nonconformities and causes, evaluating the need for preventive action, and implementing, recording, and reviewing the action taken.

■ *Internal audits* (clause 8.2.2) describes planning and conducting audits, selecting auditors, reporting results, maintaining records, and identifying the organizations responsible for taking corrective actions.

■ *Control of nonconforming product* (clause 8.3) describes how to eliminate nonconformities, take corrective actions or obtain authorization of use, release, or acceptance by the customer or relevant authority, and maintaining records of the nonconformities and actions taken.

In addition, ISO 9001 requires:

■ *Continual improvement process* (clause 8.5.1) consists of the quality policy, quality objective, audit results, analysis of data, corrective action, preventive action, and management review.

■ *Competence, training, and awareness* (clause 6.2.2) requires the organization to determine necessary competence, provide training or other actions, evaluate effectiveness of actions, ensure personnel are aware of the relevance and importance of their activities, and maintain records of education, training, skills, and experience.

4. Sandford Liebesman, "Where SOX and Your QMS Converge," *Quality Digest*, September 2007.

■ *Management review* (clause 5.6) requires the organization's management to review its management systems at planned intervals, determine opportunities for improvement, and implement needed changes. Creating a common management review process is especially important for eliminating duplicated effort and increasing communication across the organization.

The second action to link management systems is to implement ISO 9001's process approach in all of the organization's systems. The process approach, which is defined in clause 4.1 of ISO 9001, provides a basic foundation for all management systems. As applied to a linked management system environment, the process approach consists of the following activities:

■ Identify financial, quality, and environmental processes and their applications.
■ Determine the sequence and interaction of the processes.
■ Assure the operational and control effectiveness of each process.
■ Assure availability of information and resources to operate and monitor each process.
■ Monitor, measure, analyze, and continually improve each process.
■ Ensure control over outsourced processes.

In addition, the organization should:
■ Identify an owner, inputs, outputs, resources, and constraints for each process.
■ Identify financial controls for each process.
■ Identify process activities based on the plan-do-check-act (PDCA) process.
■ Implement actions to achieve planned results and improvement of processes.

The third action, where applicable[5], is to link the organization's operations to its SOX compliance process. Quality and environmental management systems provide added compliance resources that can reduce the amount of auditing time, eliminate duplicated effort, provide early identification of real-time disclosures, and support financial processes such as revenue recognition, purchasing, shipping, and inventory management. ISO 9001 provides a strong basis for managing these operations.

The fourth action is to implement the continual improvement activities defined in ISO 9001. The following will help improve operations and financial results:

---

5. Organizations that do not have to comply with SOX should still consider developing a system of internal control based on the COSO guidance.

- Use measurable objectives as improvement goals.
- Use internal audits to identify significant deficiencies in the internal controls.
- Analyze data to evaluate where continual improvement will be effective.
- Identify trends in the data to be used for early risk identification.
- Use preventive and corrective actions to reduce risk.
- Use management review to determine status of the objectives and to set new goals.

By implementing continual improvement activities, financial management will gain a better understanding of current operations. The result is a much more accurate measure of the status and effectiveness of the organization. QMS and EMS support will lead to greater transparency, continual improvement, and better bottom-line results.

An understanding of continual improvement will also help top management and the board of directors identify and control business risks. These management system processes will improve resource availability, help reduce the cost of compliance, and improve corporate governance by connecting management systems.

The fifth action is to ensure that the risk management process is complete and operating effectively. ISO 9001 includes requirements that support risk assessment. Start with the objectives and identify and analyze risks to achieving them. Identify key dependencies and significant controls and establish clear responsibility and accountability. Next, determine how to manage the risks using corrective and preventive actions. As part of these activities, the organization should develop a mechanism for dealing with change.

Chapter 3 contains an extensive description of risk management. Start with a determination of the risk appetite and risk tolerance in the organization. Risk appetite is the amount of risk, on a broad level, that an entity is willing to accept. It is the measure of the risk-reward trade-off within the business. On the other hand, risk tolerance relates to the entity's specific objectives. It is the amount of variation relative to these objectives that an entity is willing to accept. Risk tolerance varies from department to department in an organization.

Effective risk assessment requires a definition of the organization's objectives, assurance of the compatibility of its objectives, identification of risks to achieving the objectives, and judgment of which risks are critical. A common tool to use for determining the criticality of individual risks is the risk analysis matrix.

Once the risks have been identified and their criticality determined, the organization needs to identify actions to be taken. Key dependencies need to be determined, significant controls identified, and responsibilities and accountability established.

The sixth action is to conduct linked audits. This will result in a reduction in duplicated audit questions and an early assessment of operational risk. Process audits should form the backbone of the auditing program. Note that financial auditors will get a better understanding of operations, and quality and environmental auditors will get a better understanding of the financial side of the organization. A single report to the audit committee will give the members a better understanding of the organization's operations and an appreciation of the ISO 9001 and ISO 14001 management systems.

The quality, environmental, and financial audit organizations need to determine how they are the same. They need to focus on good business practices, develop linked audit schedules, expand auditor training, and be familiar with corrective and preventive action processes. They should also combine methods of identifying risks to the company. The major differences are the customers of each audit. The quality audits were provided to support compliance to ISO 9001; environmental audits support compliance to ISO 14001. They also both use audits to identify areas of improvement for operations managers. The customers of the financial audits are top management, the board of directors and third-party (regulatory) auditors.

Linked organizations need to develop methods of sharing their auditing processes. They can combine checklists, develop methods of exchanging information, and trade sampling results. The results should be shared but separate audit reports should be published.

The seventh action is to clarify the role of IT since information technology plays an important role in implementing all management systems. The IT organization must manage and protect data, as required by SOX subsections 802 and 1102. IT has a major role in controlling documents and records, managing inventory, communicating in a multisite organization, and communicating with customers and suppliers. IT must also provide an effective disaster recovery program including periodic testing of the systems. These are all functions of a QMS that support financial management, including SOX compliance. Finally, the organization can assure information security by implementing ISO/IEC 27001.

The eighth action is to improve corporate governance. There must be a separation of roles and responsibilities. The board of directors should oversee operations and assure effective corporate governance. The CEO manages the operation of the business while management supports the CEO and manages the employees.

Employees perform the functions of the organization. Three goals of corporate governance are management of risk, effective process management, and continual improvement of company performance. QMS and EMS are excellent tools for accomplishing these objectives. The board should shift the corporate mentality from correcting problems to preventing them.

The following are basic principles of good corporate governance: ensure the rights of all shareholders; recognize and protect the rights of all stakeholders; ensure timely and accurate disclosure and transparency; and define the board's responsibilities through strategic guidance, effective monitoring, and accountability. Good governance should include all the stakeholders of the organization and will develop compromises that provide the best results.

Corporate governance can be improved in a number of ways. QMS and EMS principles can be used to improve operations and reduce costs. Combined audits reports to the board can provide an understanding of the status of operations within the organization. The process approach can be used to improve organizational transparency.

Customer satisfaction data should provide valuable inputs to top management and the board of directors. Finally, QMS and EMS can be used to support the system of internal control and compliance to SOX.

8.4 CHALLENGES AND OPPORTUNITIES

QMS and EMS tools, procedures, reports, and audits are ready-made for use in a linked management system. What is lacking is the ability of the members of these management systems to communicate with each other. Few within the QMS and EMS communities understand financial statements, can communicate in financial languages, or know the requirements of SOX. There is also a need to understand how to audit for compliance to generally accepted accounting practices (GAAP)[6]. These are knowledge gaps that must be filled before effective linkage between QMS, EMS, and the financial management system can be accomplished.

How can the quality and environmental management add value to the organization? First, teach the process approach to financial management personnel. All work is based on a process and each process requires resources and contains constraints. The definition of each process should include a process owner, a descrip-

---

6. Edward Fields, *The Essentials of Finance and Accounting for Nonfinancial Managers* (American Management Association, 2002).

tion of inputs, outputs, suppliers, and customers. The suppliers and customers can be internal or external to the organization.

The process approach includes the definition of appropriate process measures or metrics and the gathering of data. Then, the data should be used to identify opportunities for process improvement and assist with the prioritization of these improvement opportunities. Next, guide the organization through process changes using good change management techniques. The end result will be an organization that's focused on continual improvement, rather than compliance.

8.5 A FINAL WORD

This book has taken you through a long journey from defining quality, environmental, and financial management systems to indicating how to link these management systems and improve the bottom line. It's up to you to bring the information to your top management.

Next time you meet with your CEO, CFO, or COO, you can use the following elevator speech:

"Sir (or Madam), I am familiar with how quality and environmental management can support financial management and break down the barriers between organizations. We need to better identify and manage risk. Quality and environmental management systems contain tools that can help with risk management and with processes that could link directly to our system of internal control mandated by SOX. I'd like the opportunity to show you how we can help."

Sarbanes-Oxley Act Index

Title 1—Public Company Accounting Oversight Board
- Section 101: Establishment and administrative provisions
- Section 102: Registration with the board
- Section 103: Auditing, quality control, independence standards, and rules
- Section 104: Inspections of registered public accounting firms
- Section 105: Investigations and disciplinary proceedings
- Section 106: Foreign public accounting firms
- Section 107: Commission oversight of the board
- Section 108: Accounting standards
- Section 109: Funding

Title II—Auditor Independence
- Section 201: Services outside the scope of practice of auditors
- Section 202: Preapproval requirements
- Section 203: Audit partner rotation
- Section 204: Auditor reports to audit committees
- Section 205: Conforming amendments
- Section 206: Conflicts of interest
- Section 207: Study of mandatory rotation of registered public accounting firms
- Section 208: Commission authority
- Section 209: Considerations by appropriate state regulatory authorities

Title III—Corporate Responsibility
- Section 301: Public company audit committees
- Section 302: Corporate responsibility for financial reports
- Section 303: Improper influence on conduct of audits
- Section 304: Forfeiture of certain bonuses and profits
- Section 305: Officer and director bars and penalties
- Section 306: Insider trades during pension fund blackout periods

- Section 307: Rules of professional responsibility for attorneys
- Section 308: Fair funds for investors

Title IV—Enhanced Financial Disclosures

- Section 401: Disclosures in periodic reports
- Section 402: Enhanced conflict of interest provisions
- Section 403: Disclosures of transactions involving management and principal stockholders
- Section 404: Management Assessment of Internal Controls
- Section 405: Exemption
- Section 406: Code of ethics for senior financial officers
- Section 407: Disclosure of audit committee financial expert
- Section 408: Enhanced review of periodic disclosures by issuers
- Section 409: Real-time issuer disclosures

Title V—Analyst Conflicts of Interest

- Section 501: Treatment of securities analysts by registered securities associations and national securities exchanges

Title VI—Commission Resources and Authority

- Section 601: Authorization of appropriations
- Section 602: Appearance and practice before the commission
- Section 603: Federal court authority to impose penny stock bars
- Section 604: Qualifications of associated persons of brokers and dealers

Title VII—Studies and Reports

- Section 701: GAO study and report regarding consolidation of public accounting firms
- Section 702: Commission study and report regarding credit rating agencies
- Section 703: Study and report on violators and violations
- Section 704: Study of enforcement actions
- Section 705: Study of investment banks

Title VIII—Corporate and Criminal Fraud Accountability

- Section 801: Short title
- Section 802: Criminal penalties for altering documents

- Section 803: Debts nondischargeable if incurred in violation of securities fraud laws
- Section 804: Statute of limitations for securities fraud
- Section 805: Review of federal sentencing guidelines for obstruction of justice and extensive criminal fraud
- Section 806: Protection for employees of publicly traded companies who provide evidence of fraud
- Section 807: Criminal penalties for defrauding shareholders of publicly traded companies.

Title IX—White-Collar Crime Penalty Enhancements
- Section 901: Short title
- Section 902: Attempts and conspiracies to commit criminal fraud offenses
- Section 903: Criminal penalties for mail and wire fraud
- Section 904: Criminal penalties for violations of the Employee Retirement Income Security Act of 1974
- Section 905: Amendment to sentencing guidelines relating to certain white-collar offenses
- Section 906: Corporate responsibility for financial reports

Title X—Corporate Tax Returns
- Section 1001: Sense of the Senate regarding the signing of corporate tax returns by chief executive officers

Title XI—Corporate Fraud and Accountability
- Section 1101: Short title
- Section 1102: Tampering with a record or otherwise impeding an official proceeding
- Section 1103: Temporary freeze authority for the Securities and Exchange Commission
- Section 1104: Amendment to the federal sentencing guidelines
- Section 1105: Authority of the commission to prohibit persons from serving as officers or directors
- Section 1106: Increased criminal penalties under Securities Exchange Act of 1934.
- Section 1107: Retaliation against informants

Case Studies

CASE STUDY 3.1: RISK MANAGEMENT AT A TEACHING HOSPITAL

Linda Ellrodt of the Juran Institute provided a case study of a major research and teaching hospital in the western United States. It has numerous locations and its quality management system (QMS) is accredited by the Joint Commission on Accreditation of Healthcare Organizations (JCAHO). The hospital's environmental management system (EMS) is registered to ISO 14001, but it's not registered to ISO 9001. Its several locations share documents and documentation online.

Management of risk

The following positions help the hospital develop and operate its risk management process:

- Hospital leadership
- Director of risk reduction
- Patient assessment personnel
- Safety squad
- Training personnel

As many health care organizations have similar processes, their risks are also similar and identified through industry groups and certification bodies such as JCAHO. Risks that are particular to a hospital—such as local requirements, financial status, or the community in general—can be brought to the hospital leadership for inclusion in the risk management process. These are typically used as input to strategic planning as well.

The risk process selected for the case study was a predefined assessment of a patient fall probability. Patient falls were selected as a key contributor to the average total length of stay (LOS) of patients. The hospital wanted to minimize LOS to control costs.

The risk of patients falling while under the hospital's care is covered under the JCAHO's National Patient Safety Goal NPSG.09.02.01[1]. This risk will be discussed as an example of an effective risk management process.

Risk of patients falling

The hospital cited two factors that effected patient falls:

- *Intrinsic factors.* Fall risk factors caused by the patient's illness or condition, such as a stroke or amputation.
- *Extrinsic factors.* Fall risk factors caused by the environment, such as a wet floor or poor lighting.

Figure B.1 Morse Falls Scale[2]		
Variables	**Numeric value**	**Score**
1. History of falling	No: 0 Yes: 25	
2. Secondary diagnosis	No: 0 Yes: 15	
3. Ambulatory aid ■ None/bed rest/nurse assist ■ Crutches/cane/walker ■ Furniture	0 15 30	
4. IV/heparin lock	No: 0 Yes: 20	
5. Gait/transferring ■ Normal/bed rest/immobile ■ Weak ■ Impaired	0 10 20	
6. Mental status ■ Oriented to own ability ■ Forgets limitations	0 15	
7. Total		

1. JCAHO's "National Patient Safety Goals," *www.jointcommission.org/PatientSafety/NationalPatientSafetyGoals/.*
2. See *www.mnhospitals.org/inc/data/tools/Safe-from-Falls-Toolkit/Morse_Fall_Scale_Assessment.doc.*

The case study examined intrinsic factors to decide on patient interventions. The hospital used the Morse Falls Scale, illustrated in figure B.1, to measure the risk likelihood of a patient falling.

The fall risk level, illustrated in figure B.2, is used to determine the risk level of falling and the action to be taken to minimize it.

Figure B.2	Fall Risk Level[3]	
Risk level	**Morse Fall Scale score**	**Action**
Low risk	0–24	Implement low-risk fall prevention interventions.
Medium risk	25–44	Implement medium-risk fall prevention interventions.
High risk	45 and higher	Implement high-risk fall prevention interventions.

The patient fall risk management process

The JCHAO[4] and the hospital objectives for reducing patient falls were to reduce liability and in-patient hospital stays. To that end, the hospital's risk assessment program for falls required it to regularly assess (and periodically reassess) each resident's risk of falling, including the potential risk associated with his or her medication regimen, and take action to address any identified risks.

Subsequently, risks were identified by the patient assessment personnel and the safety squad, who used the hospital's procedural protocols in the identification process. An example of a protocol is: "Assure enough help is provided when moving the patient or checking out the patient." The information technology (IT) organization played an important role in this process by supplying data from clinical assessments based on the protocols.[5]

Changes resulting from the risk management program

After the case study, the hospital made changes to its patient intervention and assessment tool. It was revised to include additional training on fall procedures and

---

3. Ibid.
4. "JCAHO unveils the National Patient Safety Goals, Health Care Benchmarks and Quality Improvement," *Quality Progress*, September 2004.
5. The following books can be downloaded from the JCAHO website: "Reducing the Risk of Patient Harm Resulting from Falls: Toolkit for Implementing National Patient Safety Goals" and "Good Practices in Preventing Patient Falls."

assessments, resulting in a 10-percent reduction in several categories of patient falls.

Conclusions

This case study provides an example of an organization satisfying two major types of risks: compliance risk and operational risk. The compliance risk was the loss of compliance to the JCAHO's National Safety Goals for hospitals related to patient falls. The operational risk was the lack of sufficient protocols to prevent an unacceptable number of patient falls. The hospital personnel used risk management procedures to identify these risks and to create a management process to eliminate them.

CASE STUDY 4.1: INFORMATION TECHNOLOGY MANAGEMENT AT A PROVIDER OF SPECIALIZED HEALTH MANAGEMENT SERVICES

Wes Rhea, professor at Kennesaw State University, provided a case study from his experiences as an information security officer at a company that had eight locations and about 6,000 employees.

Wes described how his organization supported supply chain management, business continuity planning (BCP), Sarbanes-Oxley (SOX) compliance, IT, and data protection. He also provided an example of a project completed by the organization: data center consolidation.

Support of supply chain management

IT personnel's role in supply chain management consisted mainly of developing software for the organization's suppliers of health management services. The risks of this process included not delivering projects on time, making changes in the scope of the projects, cost increases, and resistance to change by personnel. In some cases, the organization had to add staff or hire contractors, resulting in the need for additional training.

Business continuity planning

The IT organization was responsible for business BCP and disaster recovery (DR). It conducted interviews with key members of each business unit to determine risks and analyzes the effect of the risks. The major risks included recovery time objectives (RTO) and the costs to meet the objectives. Other concerns were the amount of resources needed, limited testing windows, and the location of call center staff during recovery. These risks gave rise to seven major priorities:

- Protection of human life and providing for employee and public safety
- Minimize confusion and indecision through advance planning and preparation.
- Minimize damage and loss of property and resources.
- Maintenance and rapid restoration of critical business operations
- Assessment of damages
- Timely return to normal business operations after an interruption
- Restoration of administration systems after an interruption

The organization's recovery project was controlled by the chief information officer (CIO) and all management and staff members were expected to fully support it. Heads of divisions and departments nominated representatives to coordinate their business recovery plan and disaster recovery process.

Support of SOX compliance

The IT organization played a supporting role in complying with the following key elements of the SOX:

- Section 103: Auditing, Quality Control, Standards and Rules
- Section 302: Corporate Responsibility for Financial Reports
- Section 404: Management Assessment of Internal Controls
- Section 409: Real-Time Issue Disclosures
- Section 802: Criminal Penalties for Altering Documents
- Section 1102: Tampering with a Record or Otherwise Impeding an Official Proceeding

IT provided evidence to show that the organization had controls for all business applications that pertain to SOX.

Information security and data protection: government regulations

There are a number of government regulations that were considered in developing the program to insure the security of information and protection of data. The Health Insurance Portability and Accountability Act (HIPPA) provides national standards for electronic health care transactions and protection of insurance for health care workers and their families when they change jobs. The law requires security and privacy of health care data.

A second regulation was the requirements of SOX that relate to protection of information. The key sections of SOX were shown in the previous section.

Finally, the third government act that was considered is the American Recovery and Reinvestment Act of 2009 (Hi-Tech Act), which is an economic stimulus package that includes funds for health care projects. There are also state data privacy laws that have to be complied with.

Data protection strategies

There were a number of strategies used by the organization to provide effective data protection: firewalls, intrusion prevention systems, virus protection, full disk encryption, and encryption of e-mails. There are also internet protocol security (IPS) and data loss protection (DLP) tools. Patch processes are used to assure accurate changes to the software used in managing data.

Awareness of data security

The final element of information security and data protection is to make employees aware of the requirements. The policies are documented and provided on the intranet. There are newsletters, e-mails, and meetings used to provide reminders and identify issues. Finally, training is provided throughout the organization using a learning management systems (LMS).

Example of IT support of a key project: data center consolidation

There were ten people on the data center consolidation project: a project manager, a data center lead, two telecom engineers, two server engineers, two network engineers, and two security engineers. They were concerned with the internal customers, the business units. The cost for the project was several million dollars, which was offset by transitioning from a third-party vendor to an in-house data center. This saved $200,000 per month. The result of the project was the ability to bring the data center in house and under the organization's direct control. The changes were implemented across the entire organization.

CASE STUDY 5.1: IMPROVING THE OPERATION OF THE DESISTI WAREHOUSE

Atul Dhanorker, an operations engineer at the Desmar Corp., provided a case study that directly links quality and financial management. Atul is currently the quality manager coordinator at the Mayo Clinic. It involves improving the inventory process, which is a key cost factor in any organization and one that financial management is especially interested in.

DeSisti Lighting, a subsidiary of Desmar Corp., is an international manufacturer of television, motion picture, and theatrical lighting and rigging equipment. The company is headquartered in Rome, Italy, with warehouse facilities in Mountainside, New Jersey. It started a Six Sigma project led by Dhanorker and illustrates the use of the define-measure-analyze-improve-control (DMAIC) methodology.

Step 1: Define the current process and the project goals

The warehouse spends a lot of time waiting for inventory to arrive from Italy and Mexico. When inventory does arrive at the warehouse, it may be incomplete or damaged. The warehouse is poorly organized and the inventory is not well preserved or accurately maintained. It's therefore difficult for the warehouse to provide distributors with accurate information on shipping dates. Customers aren't happy when their items aren't received when promised. As a result, DeSisti was losing business to its chief competitor, although it has better quality and is less expensive.

The short-term goals of DeSisti's DMAIC project were implementation of the 5S +1 process in a small section; better visual management implementation (labeling of product, shelves, etc.) in the small section; new warehouse layout with clear identification of assembly, shipping, and receiving areas; and development of a standard operating procedure (SOP) for shipping and receiving. Its long-term goals were implementation of 5S +1 in the entire warehouse; increase inventory accuracy between physical warehouse and book inventory to the industry standard of 95 percent; reduction in inventory write off by 25 percent; and reduction in warranty shipping by 25 percent.

One tool used during the define process was suppliers-inputs-process-output-customer (SIPOC) charting, which defines the steps linking a supplier input to the output to the customer. For example, in a shipment from a vendor, SIPOC consists of the vendor as the supplier, the shipment as the input, receiving as the process, inventory entry as the output, and the operations engineer as the customer. The SIPOC tool was used to define twelve warehouse subprocesses.

Closure of step one occurred after the define checklist was reviewed and the results accepted by the team.

Step 2: Measure

This step starts with the process definition, which includes measurement processes, planning, definition of critical-to-quality (CTQ) characteristics, operations definitions, sampling procedures, and analysis.

Due to a lack of proper receiving procedures, incoming goods were not checked for accuracy, shipping damage, or defects. Due to improper storage policies, some materials were lost in the warehouse and damaged or incorrect products were retrieved from storage. As part of the measure phase of DMAIC, the following CTQs were used:

■ Receiving and storage errors (the major source of inventory discrepancies)
■ Product damage
■ Incorrect lead-time information

The data used in the analysis were from October 2007–September 2008 and included inventory accuracy, returns, and warranty shipping. The sampling procedures were structured as follows:

■ A sample of 397 components
■ All the components of inventory category A (high-value items) were included.
■ The components from inventory category B (medium value) and C (low value) were included based on their sales volumes.
■ Two other sets of data were used during the analyze phase (1/1/07 through 11/14/08):
  • Warranty data
  • Return data

The data were used to find the absolute costs of inventory errors, returns, and shipping. The absolute cost of inventory error is the cost of lost orders when the inventory is missing or damaged and could be used to fulfill the orders. The cost of returns is associated with customers being dissatisfied with the product. Finally, the cost of warranty shipping is with the cost of replacing warranted products with new products.

The team also performed a cause-and-effect analysis part of a corrective action process and a value stream analysis to create the organization's desired future state.

In preparation for the analyze activity, the team also investigated the problems with tracking customer products and decided on the metrics and statistics to be used later in the process. Two baseline estimate tools used were histograms and box–and–whisker plots.

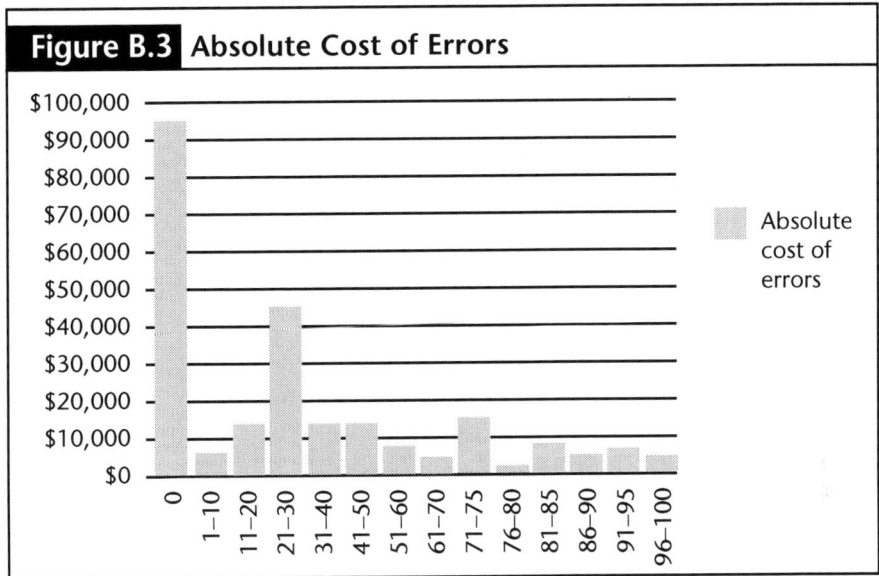

Figure B.3 illustrates a histogram with the absolute cost of errors as a function of the percent accuracy of the products. You can see that sending incorrect products to its customer was costing DeSisti a great deal of money.

Step 3: Analyze

The team used value stream mapping to identify product flow in the warehouse. It also used swim lane charts, histograms, and box-and-whisker plots to investigate problems and bottlenecks. The swim lane mapping showed each worker's activities and their interactions.

The following sequence of activities was part of the general creative solution. Process changes were identified and improvements were synthesized. A solution was selected and a pilot run in the warehouse was made and analyzed. The team considered how to expand the solution to the entire warehouse and identified possible improvements. These would be considered for a future expansion of the solution.

Figures B.4 on page 182 and B.5 on page 183 show the cost of warranties and returns. Figure B.4 shows that the largest cost of warranties is due to defective merchandise. From figure B.5, we see that the largest cost of returns is for demonstration products provided to the customers. The customers have the options of keeping these products or returning them.

Closure of step 3 occurred after the analyze phase checklist was reviewed and the results accepted by the team.

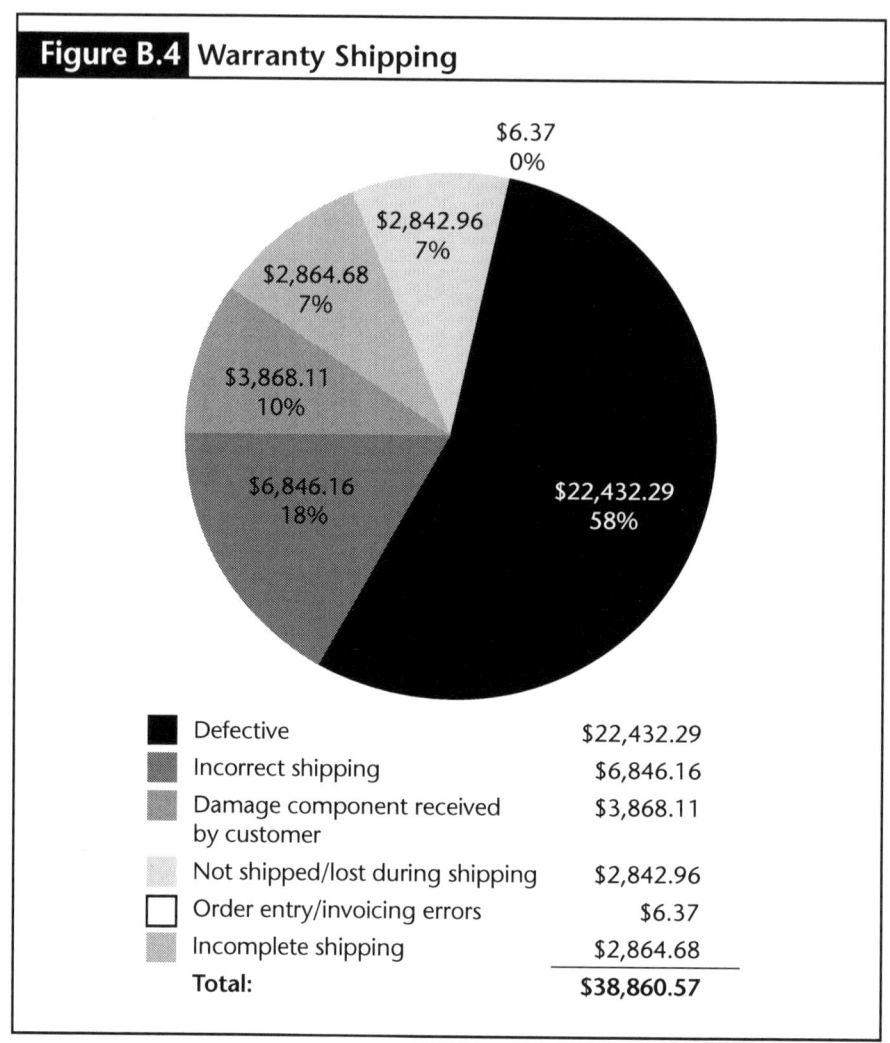

Figure B.4 Warranty Shipping

Defective	$22,432.29
Incorrect shipping	$6,846.16
Damage component received by customer	$3,868.11
Not shipped/lost during shipping	$2,842.96
Order entry/invoicing errors	$6.37
Incomplete shipping	$2,864.68
Total:	**$38,860.57**

Step 4: Improve

The first activity of the improve step was to determine the operating conditions by doing a walkthrough of the facility. An input-and-effort diagram is shown in figure B.6 on page 184.

The team then selected a 5S+1 process and labeling of shelves for implementation. The 5S methodology is based on a five-step process: sort (eliminate clutter and discard items that aren't needed regularly), set in order (organize everything), shine (clean the work area), standardize (determine best practices and standardize

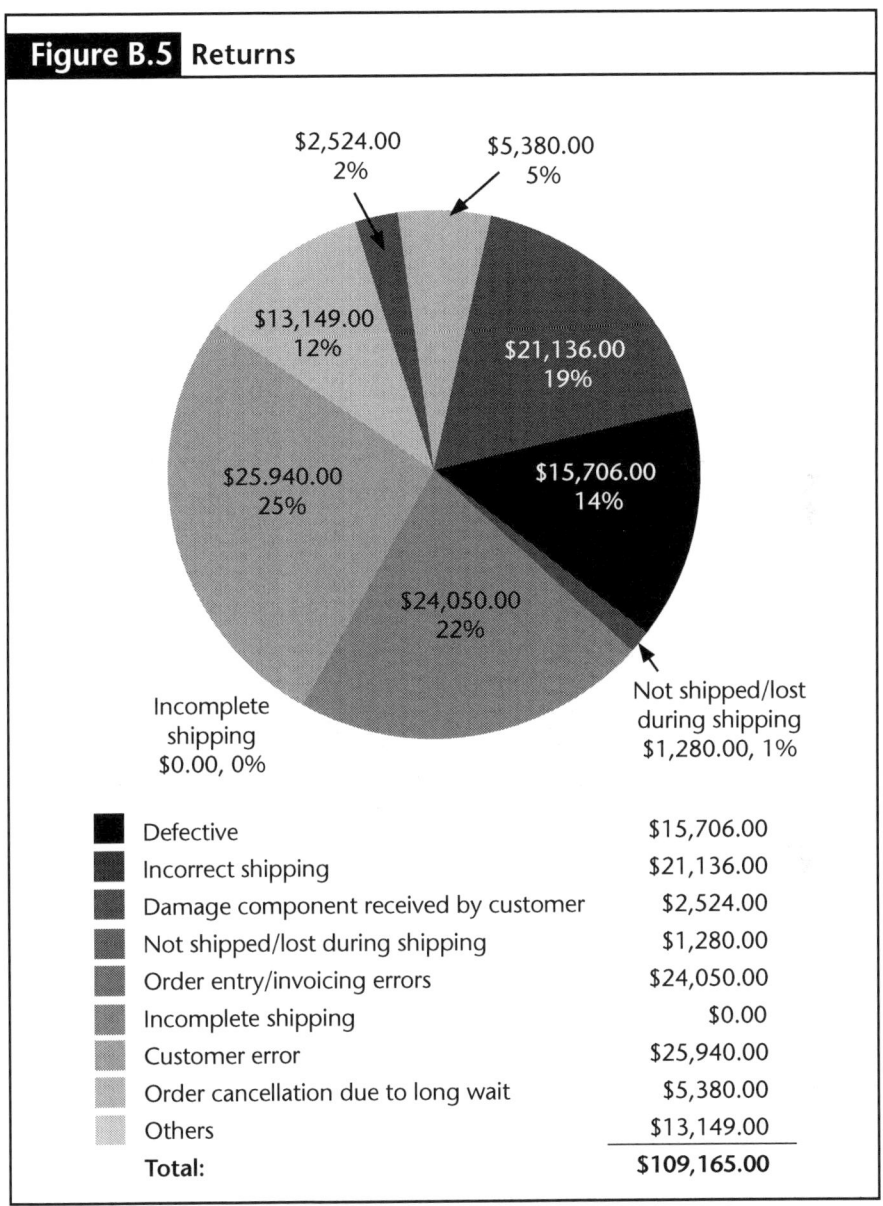

Figure B.5 Returns

■ Defective	$15,706.00
■ Incorrect shipping	$21,136.00
■ Damage component received by customer	$2,524.00
■ Not shipped/lost during shipping	$1,280.00
■ Order entry/invoicing errors	$24,050.00
■ Incomplete shipping	$0.00
■ Customer error	$25,940.00
■ Order cancellation due to long wait	$5,380.00
■ Others	$13,149.00
Total:	**$109,165.00**

them), and sustain (or self discipline, continue to keep the workplace clean and organized). 5S+1 includes attention to safety: improved signage, location of fire extinguishers, clear marking of exits and storage areas, improved lighting, and creation of safety documentation.

Figure B.6 Impact-and-Effort Diagram

Impact		Effort		
		Low	*Medium*	*High*
Impact	*High*	Shipping Procedure.	5S+1	Organize shelves.
		Receiving procedure.		Organize product.
	Medium	Label shelves.	Label items.	
		Adjust shelves.	Designate shipping and receiving area.	
			Designate assembly area.	
	Low			

Step 5: Control

The control plan consists of the following steps: standardize new methods, manage and control processes, document processes, develop standard operating procedures, revise process maps and flowcharts, and develop a response plan and process dashboards.

Other activities during the control process were: consensus building, continue to motivate associates to start and maintain 5S+1, and continue to drive concepts of Lean Six Sigma. The team used a Gantt chart to maintain a one-month cycle count. Data were also gathered on key components. Figure B.7 lists comparisons of data gathered during the project with data gathered earlier. The time frame for the second data set is about 45 percent of the first data set, which was taken into account in the analysis.

The comparison of the data indicates that the improvement in inventory management has worked well.

Conclusions

The following problem statements describe issues that arose during the DMAIC development and the improvements seen by the team.

Figure B.7	Comparison of Data in Two Time Frames		
Warranty shipping data			
Component	**10/1/07–11/14/08**	**1/1/09–7/3/09***	**Comment**
Incorrect shipping	$6,646.16	$823.49	Improvement
Damaged component received by customer	$3,868.11	$193.81	Improvement
Comparison of returns data			
	10/1/07–11/14/08	**1/1/09–7/3/09***	**Comment**
Incorrect shipping	$21,136.00	$71.50	Great improvement
Order entry/invoicing errors	$24,050.00	$236.70	Great improvement
Customer error	$25,940.00	$943.05	Great improvement

*Multiply the values in these columns by 2.22 to get the comparison.

Problem statement No. 1: There was a need for waiting time improvement. The warehouse was spending a great deal of time waiting for inventory to arrive from Italy and Mexico. When inventory did arrive it was often incomplete or damaged. Waiting time has decreased to the level of the competitor.

Problem statement No. 2: DeSisti was losing business to its major competitor even though its quality is better and its products less expensive. A comparison was made of data from July 2008 to December 2008 vs. data from January 2009 to June 2009. The results of the comparison showed that the DMAIC project had led to improvements in sales (23.80%), total number of customers (8.26%), and average order amount (28.01%). These results show the value of the DMAIC project.

Problem statement no. 3: The workplace was not well organized. A 5S+1 process was implemented throughout the entire warehouse. The process is checked monthly.

Problem statement no. 4: The warehouse inventory is not well preserved or accurately maintained. Inventory accuracy has dramatically increased, as follows:

- High-value items: Almost 100-percent accurate
- Low-value items: Approximately 90 percent accurate
- The inventory software system was improved. DeSisti no longer has difficulty finding products and boxes that are properly labeled.
- A cycle count is done every month row by row

Problem statement No. 5: The need to reduce inventory write off by 25 percent.
DeSisti wasn't able to calculate the amount of inventory write off, because it discovered a large amount of old stock that had been sent back to Mexico. It did not pursue the issue because the accounting department didn't have the resources to determine the cost savings of each stock item sent back. The positive result was the company reduced the outdated stock and recovered some of its cost.

Problem statement No. 6: The need to reduce warranty shipping by 25 percent.
This has been achieved. The major problems were due to defective components in new products. DeSisti instituted sample testing of components from suppliers. A failure of a sample leads to 100-percent inspection. Shipping errors were greatly reduced, there are fewer damages in shipping, and the number of lost shipments was reduced. Most problems were due to trucking company failures.

Finally, DeSisti has seen the following overall changes: improved warranty, shipping, and write-off costs. It has started selling used products to customers and selling demonstration products at reduced price. Overall, profit margin has increased from 27 percent to 35 percent.

CASE STUDY 5.2: (DFSS) LINKING SIX SIGMA TO FINANCIAL MANAGEMENT

Linda Ellrodt of the Juran Institute provided a case study that describes a design for Six Sigma (DFSS) success story that is linked to financial management improvement. The organization in the case study is a major U.S. cabinet maker and is registered to ISO 9001 and ISO 14001.

The organization initiated its Six Sigma program in 2003. It uses Black Belts and Green Belts, and has a Six Sigma program manager who coordinates the program and the projects. All projects are closely linked to the goals of the business and must contribute to one or more of these goals, including financial performance.

The program is very broad and utilizes many Six Sigma tools. These include critical-to-quality characteristics (CTQ) analysis, house of quality, histograms, box plots, graphs and charts, basic statistics, inferential statistics, regression analysis, design of experiments (DOE), Pareto analysis, cause-and-effect analysis, failure mode and effects analysis (FMEA), statistical process control (SPC), design scorecards, control plans, confidence intervals, data collection, analysis of variance, flow diagram, process analysis, and lessons learned.

The director of Six Sigma is responsible for the DFSS projects within the overall Six Sigma program. The quality organization provides data collection and verification of data inputs. The organization includes design projects targeted at improving service levels where significant structural changes are anticipated.

Finance/DFSS Case Study

The goal of the project was improvement of the tool used by resellers to quote projects. It consisted of improving the ergonomics of the quoting tool. The project's major customers were cabinet resellers. From a financial standpoint, this resulted in improved access to information on pricing, availability, and increased revenues.

Six Sigma Breakthrough and Beyond[6] (Juran Institute, 2003) contains a summary table of the major activities in the five phases of DFSS. It is reproduced in figure B.8.

At the completion of each phase of the project, the team met with the Six Sigma director and Juran Inc.'s consultant to review the completed actions and analysis. These phase reviews included a close examination of the statistical tools and the conclusions made. When planned and expected actions and analyses were completed, each phase was approved and closed. The project was closed when the

Figure B.8	**Major Activities in the Phases of DFSS**[7]			
Define	**Measure**	**Analyze**	**Design**	**Verify**
■ Initiate the project. ■ Scope the project. ■ Plan and manage the project.	■ Discover and prioritize customer needs. ■ Develop and prioritize CTQs. ■ Measure baseline performance.	■ Develop design alternatives. ■ Develop high-level design. ■ Evaluate high-level design.	■ Optimize detail level parameters. ■ Evaluate detail level design. ■ Plan detail design verification. ■ Verify detail and design of product. ■ Optimize process performance.	■ Execute pilot/analyze results. ■ Implement production processes. ■ Transition to owners.

6. Joseph H. DeFeo and William W. Barnard, *Six Sigma Breakthrough and Beyond* (Mc Graw-Hill, 2004).
7. Ibid

complete solution was implemented and the improvements were quantified and verified by sustained performance over a set period of time.

The five steps of define-measure-analyze-design-verify (DMADV) were accomplished as follows:

Step 1: Define

The goal of the project, as described above, was improvement of the tool used by resellers to quote projects that included the company's products.

Step 2: Measure

Resellers, the immediate customers, were looking for a comprehensive tool for creating real-time quotations to the end customers. They needed visibility into pricing, discounts, specials, and availability.

Step 3: Analyze

Resellers described a tool that would easily integrate into their way of doing business. This new tool had to be interactive, Web-based, accurate, and dependable. It was expected that resellers would provide their customers with reliable quotes for completion of the planned installation and an assessment of whether new construction or remodeling would be needed.

Step 4: Design

The company's IT department was critical to the success of this project. It created the tool and validated it through internal sales department testing.

Step 5: Verify

The tool was set up for a pilot project in an external simulation trial. After piloting and adjustments, the tool was approved for use by the network of authorized resellers and direct sales personnel.

CTQs used

Some of the CTQs used were pricing accuracy, ease of use, and visibility of product lines. The customer needs analysis was used to prioritize the CTQs for appropriately scoping the solution. The team also used the house of quality to track the solution back to the CTQs assuring that each one was addressed by the solution.

Results and lessons learned

The financial benefits of the project were $1 million in increased revenue annually. There were also a number of valuable lessons learned from the project:

- Start early and work hard.
- Start with process standardization.
- DMADV projects are more intense than DMAIC projects.
- Continuously fight scope creep and complexity.
- Manage time requirements.
- Align with the business plan.

Conclusions

The tool developed as a result of this project is now used by a nationwide network of resellers and feeds the organization's sales process. This is a good example of how Six Sigma projects work with financial management to improve the bottom line.

CASE STUDY 6.1: IMPLEMENTING A LINKED MANAGEMENT SYSTEM AT NVE CORP.

Dexter Hansen, quality assurance/information technology (QA/IT) manager of NVE Corp., provided a case study describing his organization's experience implementing a linked management system.

NVE Corp.[8] is a public organization of fifty individuals at one location that manufactures magnetic sensors (industrial, scientific, and medical applications) and couplers (isolators for commercial and industrial controls, high-end amplifiers, and communications equipment). It also licenses its magnetic random access memory technology. The company has a QMS based on ISO 9001:2008 and a financial management system based on COSO. It is not registered to an EMS.

NVE used the four-phase linked management system implementation process. The phases were planning, development, assessment, and external auditing.

Implementing phase 1: planning

The leadership team consisted of the CFO and the QA/IT manager. The procedure development was a function of the quality organization and the CFO provided review, modification, and approval of the procedures.

---

8. *www.nve.com*

The management control plan was to meet the Securities Exchange Commission (SEC) and NASDAQ SOX requirements for a small cap company. Key processes were based on application controls in three categories: inputs (transaction/ data entry procedures), processing (application processing procedures), and outputs (reports, interfacing, and distribution procedures). The control plan identified the financial processes and determined if controls existed (i.e., oversight). The company documented and modified its controls to meet compliance requirements based on COSO and good accounting and audit practices. Also included in the control plan was a review of IT practices and controls as they related to requirements.

The control objectives were to lower risks, ensure control, maintain oversight, and provide auditable evidence of compliance and control. The risks of not satisfying the objectives were possible losses due to fraud, theft, or noncompliance to contracts. The organization is subject to audits by the federal government due to small business innovation research (SBIR) and other contracts. Noncompliance with SOX section 404 could result in fines and/or incarceration of company executives.

The following processes were included in the control plan: accounts receivable, accounts payable, cash and investment management, production and inventory control, sales order entry, and order acceptance and shipping.

Phase 1 was completed after review, modification, and approval by the CFO.

Implementing phase 2: Development

During the development phase, the organization expanded the analysis of its financial, quality, and environmental management processes and procedures. The lessons learned from phase 1 and the resulting analysis were used to revise the organization's procedures and related documentation. The organization also used existing controls to minimize business risks.

An effective IT infrastructure is vital to a working operating system. As part of phase 2, the IT system infrastructure was reviewed against the COSO and CobIT[9] frameworks.

During phase 2, the quality manual was updated, financial and quality process descriptions were improved, and flowcharts were revised. Personnel responsible for the provision of products and services were trained in ISO 9001's changes and internal controls, a SOX Web course was created to train all employees, and a

---

9. See "CobIT Management of IT Controls" in chapter 4.

"tone of the company" survey was conducted to assure effective management involvement as part of the SOX review. Phase 2 was completed after review, modification, and approval by the CFO.

Implementing phase 3: internal assessment

The financial and quality internal auditors developed a linked audit plan that included the following:

■ Linkages between ISO 9001 and COSO
■ Identification of key controls
■ Evaluation of internal controls at the entity and activity levels
■ Evaluation of internal controls at service providers, only as far as they affected NVE procedures
■ Testing the controls
■ Documentation of the audit results

A linked internal audit was completed based on the audit plan. Corrective actions resulted in minor procedural changes and changes to the IT processes including the addition of off-site backup for financial records.

Phase 3 was completed with the documentation of the internal audit results and corrective and preventive actions.

Implementing phase 4: external auditing

Preparation for the external audit was based on the organization's internal audit procedures. This included the use of checklists from that audit and review of the system of internal control. NVE also used experience from government and ISO 9001 audits. Training was focused on ensuring that procedures would be followed correctly. As a result of this preparation, NVE passed its external audits without any material findings.

Lessons learned from this case study

NVE implemented changes across the organization as a result of the internal and external audits. This included securing the IT network and the IT procedures. It also separated its accounts payable and accounts receivable functions and clarified the duties of financial personnel.

CASE STUDY 6.2: IMPLEMENTING A LINKED MANAGEMENT SYSTEM AT STONCOR GROUP INC.

Tom Carpenter, director of corporate compliance at the Stonhard division of StonCor Group Inc. of Maple Shade, New Jersey, provided a case study describing his organization's experience implementing a linked management system. StonCor is an organization of 2,370 employees at sixteen locations that manufactures and installs corrosion protection products and polymer flooring and coatings. It is part of RPM International Inc., a public company listed on the New York Stock Exchange.

The Stonhard division has a QMS based on ISO 9001:2000 and a financial management system based on a combination of the Hyperion and SOX systems. StonCor used the SOX legislation as a guideline for this integration to ensure that its legal requirements were met.

Part of the organization also uses the Baldrige Criteria and StonCor has an EMS that is in the process of being registered to ISO 14001:2004.

Implementing phase 1: planning

The leadership team consisted of the president and department vice presidents. They were involved with the development from the beginning of the project. The finance organization wrote the procedures and controls used to address SOX requirements based on templates provided by the parent organization. Finance wasn't involved in building the QMS during the mid-1990s, but was involved in the integration of the two systems when SOX appeared.

The control plan was developed during this phase with the objectives of standardizing processes and minimizing losses from nonconforming products. The following were the key processes defined in the control plan:

- Document control
- Corrective and preventive actions
- Material review boards
- Internal auditing

The control plan was originally developed with sales and manufacturing as the internal customers. More recently, this has been expanded to all areas of the corporation. The goals of the plan were focused on financial, quality, and environmental issues. The financial goals were to lower repair costs and reduce waste disposal. For quality, it was standardization of manufacturing and test processes and better control and oversight of specifications. The environmental goals were the reduction of waste generation and lowering of disposal costs.

Phase 1 was over when the plans were completed that linked the QMS to SOX.

Implementing phase 2: development

During the development phase, the organization expanded its documentation of its financial, quality, and environmental management processes and procedures. The ISO 9001 manual was revised and the ISO 14001 manual was created. These manuals include descriptions of the internal control system and their relationships to ISO 9001 and ISO 14001. Other documentation was developed in support of these relationships.

For SOX compliance, narratives were developed that provided details of how each accounting-related function was performed. Potential risks for each process were identified and controls were originated to address each of the risks. Where a control could not immediately be developed for a risk, a "gap" was identified. The gaps were subsequently closed when the control was fully in place.

ISO 9001, ISO 14001, and internal controls training was provided in level 2 documentation and the quality and environmental management manuals. Records were kept of all personnel who completed the training.

Phase 2 was completed based on compliance to ISO 9001 and satisfaction of the SOX requirements.

Implementing phase 3: internal assessment

The financial, quality, and environmental internal auditors developed a linked audit plan that included the following:
- Identification of key controls
- Evaluation of internal controls at the entity and activity levels
- Evaluation of internal controls at service providers
- Testing the controls
- Documenting the audit results
- Evaluation of internal controls at supply organizations
- Documenting the results of corrective actions

A linked internal audit was completed based on the audit plan. The results of the audit indicated that all required systems, processes, and procedures have been implemented and are functioning as planned.

Phase 3 was completed with the documentation of the internal audit results and the corrective actions.

Implementing phase 4: external auditing

The major preparation for the external audits was based on the internal audit procedures. This included the use of the checklists from that audit and the review of the system of internal control. Personnel were trained on how to interact with the auditors. StonCor has had no major findings during its last three third-party audits.

Lessons learned from this case study

The following are critical lessons learned: involvement of key personnel from the very start from all affected areas, training and continual retraining of personnel is essential, and timely follow-up must be done when problems are identified. It was also vital that StonCor corrected processes that couldn't be followed as written. Training was provided on processes that weren't followed.

The bottom line was that StonCor changed the culture of its organization from management by fear to management by cooperation and mutual respect.

Definitions and Acronyms

Accounts payable: What the company owes suppliers for products and services it has already received.

Accounts receivable: Amount owed to the company by its customers for products and services it has provided.

Amortization: An accounting process for spreading an investment over the years of its useful life. For a loan, the method of monthly payments including principle and interest.

Balance sheet: Measures the financial health and liquidity of the business over time. The balance sheet covers the following: current and long-term assets, and liabilities consisting of accounts payable, taxes, and short-term debt. Equity = total assets – total liabilities.

Cash flows: The statement of cash flow describes day-to-day business operations. It reflects the flow of activity in the profit-and-loss statement and the balance sheet during day-to-day business operations (exclusive of investing and financing). There are three types of cash flows: operations, investments, and financing.

Corporate governance: The relationship between management, the board of directors, shareholders, and other stakeholders. These relationships create the structure through which the objectives of the company are set, attained, and monitored.

Cost of goods sold (COGS): The costs associated with raw materials, purchased components, direct labor, operating and repairing manufacturing equipment, and other manufacturing expenses (utilities, maintaining the facilities, etc.).

Economic value added (EVA): The result of: (return on capital – cost of capital) × (capital invested)

Earnings before interest and taxes (EBIT): Operating revenue – operating expenses + nonoperating income. Operating expenses includes COGS, selling, general, and administrative expenses (SG&A); depreciation; amortization; and other expenses.

EBITDA = EBIT + (depreciation and amortization)

Financial controls: Processes designed to provide assurance regarding the reliability of financial reporting and the preparation of financial statements. They are prepared in accordance with general accepted accounting principles (GAAP). Key controls are controls over transactions that ensure the accuracy of financial statement assertions.

General ledger: Where all accounting transactions are ultimately recorded and the data source for most basic financial statements. The general ledger must always be in balance. Total assets must equal total liabilities.

Internal control: A process designed by an entity's board of directors, management, and other personnel to provide reasonable assurance regarding the achievement of objectives in the following categories: effectiveness and efficiencies of operations, reliability of financial reporting, and compliance with applicable laws and regulations.

Internal control deficiencies: The design or operation of a control doesn't allow management or employees to prevent or detect misstatements on a timely basis in the normal course of performing their assigned functions. Examples of this include: a control objective is missing or an existing control is not properly designed so that—even if the control operates as designed—the control objective would not be met. A deficiency in operation exists when a properly designed control doesn't operate as designed or when the person performing the control doesn't possess the necessary authority or competence to perform the control effectively.

Material weakness: A deficiency or a combination of deficiencies in internal control over financial reporting, such that there is a reasonable possibility that a material misstatement of the company's annual or interim financial statements won't be prevented or detected on a timely basis. Examples include a lack of controls in place to ensure reconciliation of internal material transfers such as inventory transfers, allocation of research and development costs, corporate charges, and frequent failure of a single-source supplier to ship key components, resulting in major losses of business.

Net present value (NPV): The cash flow of the investment in a project discounted to reflect the time value of money.

Operating income: Revenue – COGS – gross profit – SG&A expenses – depreciation – amortization.

Price/earnings ratio: (Common stock price) / (earnings per share)

Profit-and-loss statement: A measure of the performance of a business at a point in time. It consists of measuring income and expenses. Income consists of revenues and earnings, and expenses include COGS, operating expenses, SG&A expenses, depreciation, amortization, capital expenses, income tax, and other expenses.

Revenue recognition: A financial term that can affect costs and profits. It consists of tracing products from sales through production, to delivery and payments received.

Return on investments (ROI): Profit/average investment

Return on equity (ROE): Profit/average shareholder equity

Significant deficiency: A control deficiency or combination of control deficiencies that adversely affects a company's ability to initiate, authorize, record, process, or report external financial data reliability in accordance with generally accepted accounting principals such that a misstatement of the company's annual or interim financial statements that is more than inconsequential will not be prevented or detected. Examples include ineffective oversight of external financial reporting and internal controls over financial reporting by the audit committee; material misstatements in the financial statements not initially identified by internal controls; significant deficiencies reported to management and the audit committee that remain uncorrected after a reasonable period of time; ineffective oversight of external financial reporting and internal controls over financial reporting by the audit committee; material misstatements in the financial statements not initially identified by internal controls; and a lack of controls in place to ensure reconciliation of all internal accounting, such as cash transfers from one department to another regardless of transaction size.

Tone at the top: The ethical atmosphere that is created in the workplace by the organization's leadership. Whatever tone management sets will have a trickle-down effect on employees.

ACRONYMS

- AICPA: American Institute of Certified Public Accountants
- ANOV: Analysis of variance
- BCP: Business continuity planning
- CFO: Chief financial officer
- CIO: Chief information officer
- COBIT: Control objectives for information and related technology
- COSO: Committee of Supporting Organizations of the Treadway Commission. Also used for the documents providing COSO guidance.
- CTQ: Critical to quality
- DFSS: Design for Six Sigma
- DMADV: Define-measure-analyze-design-verify
- DMAIC: Define-measure-analyze-improve-control
- DOE: Design of experiments
- ERM: Enterprise risk management

- ERP: Enterprise resource planning
- FASB: Financial Accounting Standards Board
- FMEA: Failure mode and effects analysis
- FMS: Financial management systems
- GAAP: Generally Accepted Accounting Practices
- IFA: Internal financial auditor
- IIA: Institute of Internal Auditors
- IMA: Institute of Management Accountants
- ISO: International Organization for Standardization
- IT: Information technology
- JCAHO: Joint Commission on Accreditation of Healthcare Organizations
- LSS: Lean Six Sigma
- ORCA: Objectives, risk, controls, and alignment process
- PCAOB: Public Company Accounting Oversight Board
- PDCA: Plan-do-check-act
- P&L: Profit-and-loss statement
- QMS/EMS: Quality and environmental management systems
- SCM: Supply chain management
- SEC: Securities and Exchange Commission
- SOX: Sarbanes-Oxley Law

Appendix D

SAS 70 Auditing Standard

The SAS 70 auditing standard for service organizations is a widely recognized standard developed by the American Institute of Certified Public Accountants (AICPA). A successful SAS 70 audit indicates that a service organization has completed an in-depth audit of its control objectives and control activities. This often includes controls over information technology and related processes. The requirements of section 404 of the Sarbanes-Oxley Act of 2002 make SAS 70 audit reports even more important to the process of reporting on the effectiveness of internal control over financial reporting.

SAS 70 provides guidance to enable an independent auditor ("service auditor") to issue an opinion on a service organization's description of controls through a Service Auditor's Report. There are two types of Service Auditor's Reports: A Type I report describes the service organization's description of controls at a specific point in time (e.g., June 30, 2009). A Type II report not only includes the service organization's description of controls, but also includes detailed testing of its controls over a minimum six-month period (e.g., January 1, 2009 to June 30, 2009).

Service and supply organizations receive significant value from having a SAS 70 engagement performed. A Service Auditor's Report with an unqualified opinion that is issued by an independent accounting firm differentiates the organization from its peers by demonstrating the establishment of effectively designed control objectives and control activities. The Service Auditor's Report also helps the organization build trust with its customers.

User organizations that obtain a SAS 70 report from their suppliers receive valuable information regarding that organization's controls and their effectiveness. In a Type II report, the user organization receives a detailed description of the controls and an independent assessment of whether the controls were placed in operation, suitably designed, and operating effectively.

Bibliography

Books

Arthur, Jay *Lean Six Sigma Demystified* (Mc Graw-Hill, 2007)

Anand, Sanjay *The Sarbanes-Oxley Act, An Introduction* (Van Haren Publishing, 2008)

Cobb, Charles G. *From Quality to Business Excellence* (ASQ Quality Press, 2003)

Campanella, Jack *Principles of Quality Costs, Principles, Implementation and Use, Third Edition* (ASQ Quality Press, 1999)

DeFeo, Joseph A. and William W. Barnard *Six Sigma Breakthrough and Beyond* (McGraw-Hill, 2004)

Ditech Networks *Management Information Systems Manual*

Fields, Edward *The Essentials of Finance and Accounting for Nonfinancial Managers* (American Management Association, 2002)

George, Michael L. *Lean Six Sigma: Combining Six Sigma Quality with Lean Speed* (McGraw-Hill, 2002)

George, Michael L. *Lean Six Sigma for Service* (McGraw-Hill, 2003)

Gleim, Irvin N. and Wlliam A. Hillison *Gleim's CPA Review, Auditing* (Gleim Publications Inc., 2001)

Green, Scott *Manager's Guide to the Sarbanes-Oxley Act* (John Wiley & Sons Inc., 2004)

Harry, Mikel and Richard Schroeder *Six Sigma: The Breakthrough Strategy Revolutionizing the World's Top Corporations* (Currency, 2000)

Hayler, Rowland and Nichols, Michael D *Six Sigma for Financial Services* (McGraw-Hill, 2007)

Hutchins, Greg *Value-Added Auditing* (Quality Plus Engineering, 2003)

The Institute of Internal Auditors *Sarbanes-Oxley Section 404: A Guide for Management by Internal Control Practitioners* (The Institute of Internal Auditors, 2006)

The Institute of Internal Auditors *The ALLTELL Control and Risk Self-Assessment Processes* (The Institute of Internal Auditors, 2004)

Kaplan, Robert S. and David P. Norton *The Balanced Scorecard* (Harvard Business School Press, 1996)

Land, Susan K. and John W. Walz *Practical Support for CMMI-SW Software Project*

Documentation Using IEEE Software Engineering Standards (John Wiley & Sons, 2005)

Lander, Guy P. *What is Sarbanes-Oxley?* (McGraw-Hill, 2004)

Meisel, Robert M., Steven J. Babb, Steven F Marsh, and James P. Schlichting *The Executive Guide to Understanding and Implementing Lean Six Sigma: The Financial Impact* (ASQ Quality Press, 2007)

Palmes, Paul C. *Process-Driven Comprehensive Auditing, Second Edition* (ASQ Quality Press, 2009)

Pyzdek, Thomas *The Six Sigma Handbook* (McGraw-Hill, 2003)

Siciliano, Gene *Finance for the Non-Finance Manager* (McGraw-Hill, 2003)

Stimson, William A. *ISO 9001 & Sarbanes-Oxley: A System of Governance* (Paton Press, 2006)

Stoner, James A. F. and Frank M. Werner *Managing Finance for Quality* (ASQ Quality Press, 1994)

Torok, Robert M. and Patrick J. Cordon *Operational Profitability: Systematic Approaches for Continuous Improvement Second Edition* (John Wiley & Sons Inc., 2002)

Treichler, David M. and Ronald D. Charmichael *The Six Sigma Path to Leadership* (American Society for Quality, 2004)

Watkins, Steve *ISO 27001: a Pocket Guide* (IT Governance Publications, 2007)

Weaver, Samuel C. and J. Fred Weston *Finance and Accounting for Nonfinancial Managers* (Mc-Graw-Hill, 2001)

Weston, Fred Finance *Accounting for Nonfinancial Managers* (McGraw-Hill, 2001)

Womack, James P. and Daniel T. Jones *Lean Solutions* (Free Press, 2005)

Standards

ISO 9000:2005 Quality Management Systems—Fundamentals and Vocabulary, (International Organization for Standardization, 2005)

ISO 9001:2008 Quality Management Systems—Requirements, (International Organization for Standardization, 2008)

ISO 10014: 2006 Quality Management Systems—A Guideline for Realizing Financial and Economic Benefits, (International Organization for Standardization, 2006)

ISO 14001:2004, Environmental Management Systems—Requirements With Guidance for Use, (International Organization for Standardization, 2004)

ISO 14971, Medical Devices—Application of Risk Management to Medical Devices, (International Organization for Standardization, 2007)

ISO/IEC 27001:2005 Information technology—Security Techniques—Specification for an Information Security Management System, (International Organization for Standardization, 2005)

ISO/IEC 27002:2005 Information technology—Security Techniques—Code of Practice for Information Security Management, (International Organization for Standardization, 2005)

ISO/IEC 27006:2007 Information Technology—Security Techniques—Requirements for Bodies Providing Audit and Certification of Information Security Management Systems," (International Organization for Standardization, 2007)

CobIT 4.1, Control Objectives for Information and Related Technology, (IT Governance Institute, 2007)

Quality System Inspection Technique (QSIT), (U.S. Food and Drug Administration, August 1999)

Articles

Alukal, George "Create a Lean Mean Machine" (*Quality Progress,* April 2003)

Carlson, Carl S. "FMEA Success Factors: An Effective FMEA Process" (*Reliability Edge,* Volume 6, Issue 1)

Liebesman, Sandford, Paul Palmes, and John Walz "Use Management Tools to Mitigate Risk from SOX" (*The Informed Outlook,* January 2004)

Liebesman, Sandford "Quality Practitioners and Effective Corporate Governance" (*Quality Progress,* March 2004)

Liebesman, Sandford "Mitigate SOX Risk with ISO 9001 and 14001" (*Quality Progress,* September 2005)

Liebesman, Sandford "Quality in the Mix" (*Internal Auditor,* October 2005)

Liebesman, Sandford "QMSs and EMSs Support Financial Management Systems" (*Quality Progress,* March 2006)

Liebesman, Sandford "Where SOX and Your QMS Converge" (*Quality Digest,* September 2007)

Liebesman, Sandford "ASQ Team Says QMS and EMS Standards Support SOX" (*Quality Progress,* October 2007)

Liebesman, Sandford "How to Manage Risk in a Global Economy" (*Quality Progress,* March 2008)

Liebesman, Sandford "Down with Silos" (*Quality Progress,* September 2008)

McDonald, Mary, Terry A. Mors, and Ann Phillips "Management System Integration: Can it be Done?" (*Quality Progress,* October 2003)

Welborn, Cliff "Using FMEA to Assess Outsourcing Risk" (*Quality Progress,* August 2007)

Websites

American Accounting Association: *www.aaa-edu.org*

American Institute of Certified Public Accountants: *www.aicpa.org*

ASQ SOX Community: *www.asq.org/communities/sox/index.html*

Committee of Sponsoring Organizations: *www.coso.org*

Ditech Networks: *www.ditech.com*

Financial Executives International: *www.fei.org*

The Institute of Internal Auditors: *www.theiia.org*

Institute of Management Accountants: *www.imanet.org*

IT Governance Institute: *www.itgi.org*

Minitab: *www.minitab.com*

Protiviti: *www.protiviti.com*

Public Company Accounting Oversight Board: *www.pcaobus.org*

Revenue Recognition: *www.revenuerecognition.com*

U.S. Food and Drug Administration: *www.fda.gov*

Index

V

value stream 82, 180
   value stream mapping 84, 92, 181
value-to-waste ratio 84
Van Putten, Dirk xiii– xiv
variance analysis 8
Visio 97
visual communication 85
VOC
   see voice of the customer
voice of the customer 88–89, 92

W

Walz, John xiii
Wang, Will xiv
waste 4–5, 9, 81–85, 127
   eight types of wastes 82–83
      delays in production 83
      excess inventory 82
      excess movement 82
      overprocessing 83
      overproduction 83
      poor-quality costs 83
      underutilization of personnel 83
      wasted motion 83
   enterprise resource planning 60
   environmental waste 35, 60, 192–193
   financial goals 192
   implement phase 2, 127
   Lean Six Sigma 4, 5, 9, 13, 81, 85, 159
   lean tools 84
Welch, Jack 85
Welsch, Tom xiv
whistleblower 18, 20, 62–63
   protection 15

white-collar crime penalty enhancement 16, 19, 171
Womack, James P. 82
Woodbridge Group xiv, 143
WorldCom 15–16